eMinistry

eMinistry

Connecting with the Net Generation

ANDREW CAREAGA

kregel
PUBLICATIONS

Grand Rapids, MI 49501

eMinistry: Connecting with the Net Generation

© 2001 by Andrew Careaga

Published by Kregel Publications, a division of Kregel, Inc., P.O. Box 2607, Grand Rapids, MI 49501. Kregel Publications provides trusted, biblical publications for Christian growth and service. For more information about Kregel Publications, visit our web site: www.kregel.com

ISBN 0-8254-2370-8

Printed in the United States of America

2 3 4 5 / 05 04 03 02

Contents

A New Church for a New World

THE SOCIAL AND RELIGIOUS revolution created by the Internet is the great untold story of our day. It is an even greater story than the beginning-to-be-told story of the Internet's technological revolution.

I let my fingers do the walking. My kids have Web feet. They don't go anywhere without first going to the Web. The invention that is fashioning the future is the Internet, the fastest-growing technology the world has ever known.

In the past thirty years the Internet has gone from something nonexistent to something nobody took seriously to the driving force of the dawning world. Two million new Web pages of pavement are being laid every day, a superhighway transporting a global renaissance of innovation and invention. Think what the next twenty, fifty, or seventy-five years will bring. Like the printing press before it, the Internet is forcing us to rewrite the rules of every game.

The Internet is splitting us all into two cultural camps: immigrants and natives. If you're over thirty-eight you're an immigrant. If you're under thirty-eight you're a native. Natives have a whole new mind-set. Native culture is creating new keys, new questions, new answers, new rules, even a new church.

My favorite story about the differing worlds of immigrants and natives is the announcement by Pierre Salinger of his discovery of what brought down TWA Flight 800 from the skies and into the waters off the Atlantic Coast.

Salinger called a news conference to announce his discovery that it was a test missile fired by U.S. military that went astray and blew up the passenger aircraft. Because it was Pierre Salinger—author, former presidential press secretary, ambassador to France, and so forth—the news media showed up in force. CNN carried the press conference live as Salinger stood on the beach where the wreckage had washed ashore and passed out the "proof" for his findings that a misguided missile exploded the airplane.

After skimming one document quickly, a news correspondent asked, "Where did you get this?"

"I downloaded it from the Internet."

"Where did *this* document come from?" asked another reporter.

"I got that from the Internet, too."

Within a few long minutes, it became apparent that all of Salinger's "proof" had been collated from various Web sites. The news conference came to an abrupt conclusion.

Salinger grew up in a book culture where, if information made it into print, it had been juried, refereed, cross-referenced, edited, copyedited, and reviewed by critics. Unless something was self-published by some "vanity press," you could trust the information, albeit what you did with the interpretation was up to you.

Salinger unwittingly found himself an immigrant in a world where everyone is an author, everyone a publisher, and everyone an expert. The blessing of the Internet is that it contains everything. The curse of the Internet is that it contains everything. Natives need bibliographic and hermeneutic skills in grade school that immigrants didn't need until college and graduate school. The mistake of applying one medium's standards to another medium is now known as "The Salinger Syndrome."

"There's the bit where you say it," admits J. L. Austin, "and the bit where you take it back." Now that I've said it, let me take it back a bit.

Being a "native" or being an "immigrant" is more a mind-set than a matter of chronology, more psychographics than demographics, more a spirit than a matter of geriatrics and pediatrics. I know of some eighty- and ninety-year-olds who have more of a native head-set than some twenty- and thirty-year-olds.

In fact, the Internet is really the biggest bequest of immigrants. It was invented and designed by boomers, former flower-power children of the 1960s, most of whom never profited from its discovery. In fact, the early architects of the Web were opposed to any commercial uses of their creation, which was loosely organized in good commune fashion. They believed in "open source" movements, and commercial application was not an "acceptable-use policy." The Internet was developed and commercialized by the native children of idealistic immigrants (Bezos, Yang, Andreesen), who made fortunes where their parents made fantasies.

The biggest question facing the Christian church today is this: Will it require de-nativization for membership in the body of Christ, or will it indigenize the gospel in native culture? It's a question that every arena of life is facing, from economics to literature.

It's a WWW world. I know of no better guide to this new world than Andrew Careaga. His earlier book, *E-vangelism,* is required reading for my divinity students. This book dealing with electronic ministry is a wake-up call to a church that still requires natives to become like immigrants if they are to embrace Christianity. Careaga shows how a biblically faithful relationship with Christ can be facilitated through digital technology.

If the archangel Gabriel himself came down and told us about a new church for a new world, I can't imagine how he would have said it any differently.

—LEONARD SWEET
Drew University

Preface

IN THE PROCESS OF conducting research for this book, the author interviewed dozens of teenagers via electronic mail or chats and gathered information from several online forums. To preserve the integrity of these N-Geners' online voices, and to provide the reader with a sense of how N-Geners communicate in cyberspace, the author has made no attempt to edit or correct spelling or punctuation errors. For this reason, the reader may encounter typographical and grammatical errors in quoted materials, as well as many nontraditional spellings that are commonplace in the online venues of chat rooms and Internet newsgroups.

The author has made every attempt to verify the addresses of all Web sites and online forums cited in this book. In the ever-changing world of cyberspace, however, Web denizens often move on, without leaving a forwarding address. For that reason, readers might encounter references to Web sites and other online resources that have changed since publication. The best way to find updates is by going online and typing the Web site or forum title into a reliable search engine.

Acknowledgments

WRITING THIS BOOK has made me appreciate the wisdom of Benjamin Disraeli's claim that "the best way to become acquainted with a subject is to write a book about it." Certainly, that claim holds true in this instance. But books, even the best of books, make poor substitutes for encounters with real people. While I've tried my best to describe and portray the Net Generation herein, I could never have done it without making the acquaintance of some very special and talented people.

My research led me to seek out theologians; trendspotters; fellow writers and youth ministers; online missionaries; scores of teenagers; and dozens of Internet surfers, searchers, and cybersaints. All of my online and offline encounters, whether deliberate on my part or (quite often) serendipitous, have helped to shape this book. Several individuals in particular provided guidance, inspiration, encouragement, and wisdom along the way, and I would like to thank them for their contributions toward making this book a reality.

My wife, Dyann Careaga, is always by my side. Throughout this project, she demonstrated great patience as I spent too many long evenings at the computer. I thank her for her love, patience, and encouragement.

I'm grateful for the wisdom and friendship of many online friends whom I've never met face-to-face, among them Tony Whittaker and David Campbell, true "men of Issachar" (1 Chron. 12:32 NIV) for our time. I'm also grateful to smiling cybersaint Peggie Bohanon, the executive editor of *Internet for Christians* newsletter, whom I finally got to meet face-to-face. Leonard Sweet has been my Barnabas throughout this project, lending an encouraging word just when it was needed. The ministry and congregation at Salem Faith Assembly Church continue to be a constant source of encouragement and love for me. In particular, I wish to thank the *ALIENS* youth ministry at Salem Faith for giving me a reality check on a weekly basis.

Finally, I wish to thank the many N-Geners who have opened their world to me and shown me its beauty and wonder. May God's grace fill them and envelop them as they live out the story of their lives.

Introduction

Out of the mouth of babes and sucklings hast thou or-
dained strength.

—Psalm 8:2 KJV

IN SHERRY TURKLE'S BOOK *The Second Self: Computers and the Hu-*
man Spirit, a twelve-year-old named David explains his views about
the future of artificial intelligence:

> When there are computers who are just as smart as people,
> the computers will do a lot of the jobs, but there will still
> be things for the people to do. They will run the restau-
> rants, taste the food, and they will be the ones who will
> love each other, have families and love each other. I guess
> they'll still be the ones who will go to church.[1]

In the decade and a half since David's observation, the state of
computer technology has advanced far beyond anything imagined
in the mid-1980s. Today, a new kind of church is emerging for
people to attend. The global hive of interconnected computers
known as the Internet is the "Roman Road" network of our day,
connecting the body of Christ in ways never before possible. In

scores of Internet chat rooms, people *and* computers now "go to church" together. It is not the kind of church to which most of us are accustomed. Nevertheless, people—and perhaps computers?— *are* experiencing worship within these Internet churches. And young people, especially teenagers, are often leading these online congregations—with the assistance of their computer software programs, of course.

JesusFrk and the Virtual Bible

One evening, I discovered a few of the faithful cyber-congregants gathered in a chat room called *#ChristianTeens*. No one in this virtual sanctuary was preaching a sermon or singing praises to God. Instead, what they were doing resembled a cyberspace version of a Bible drill, with "f|owrpowr" and "Drake" quizzing a *#ChristianTeens* regular named "JesusFrk" on his knowledge of Scripture.

But JesusFrk is no typical Bible student. On my screen, JesusFrk appeared as simply one of seven ASCII nicknames listed down the right-hand side of the "window" that connects me to this virtual room. Other than the @ symbol appearing before the nickname, indicating JesusFrk's status as a channel administrator or operator ("op"), JesusFrk looked no different than any other member of the chat room.

Unlike f|owrpowr and Drake, however, JesusFrk is not the textual representation of a human being. JesusFrk is a computer program. He (or rather *it*) is a virtual robot, or "Bible bot," an automated software program that spews Bible verses—in either the King James or the New International versions, depending on the user's preference—onto chatters' computer screens on command, as f|owrpowr demonstrated:

```
<f|owrpowr> $niv matthew 14:3
<JesusFrk> Matthew 14:3 Now Herod had arrested
John and bound him and put him in prison because
of Herodias, his brother Philip s wife (NIV)
```

Reasonably impressed, Drake took JesusFrk out for a spin, tossing this Bible bot a few random chapter-verse citations.

```
<Drake> $niv acts 13:12
<JesusFrk> Acts 13:12 When the proconsul saw
what had happened, he believed, for he was amazed
at the teaching about the Lord. (NIV)
<Drake> these are just random . . .
<Drake> that is so cool
<Drake> $kjv proverbs 3:22
<JesusFrk> [Proverbs 3:22] So shall they be
life unto thy soul, and grace to thy neck. (KJV)
<Drake> woohoo
```

Generation Net

Drake and f|owrpowr are members of a new generation of young Christians—the Internet Generation—who are exploring and expressing their faith in this strange new world of cyberspace. JesusFrk is the resident Bible bot for #ChristianTeens, one of dozens of Christian chat channels that exist in the virtual venue of Internet Relay Chat (IRC). For Drake, f|owrpowr, and other members of the Net Generation, the Bible bot is as integral a part of the faith experience as hymnals and pews were to an earlier generation of believers.

As access to the Internet continues to increase, more people—young and old alike and both Christian and non-Christian—are logging on to the Net in their quest for meaning. Chat networks such as the Undernet and Dalnet allow people from all over the world to do that with ease. In this virtual world, they visit, debate, discuss issues, engage in Christian fellowship, and even hold Bible studies. If the room happens to have a Bible bot (and many Christian chat rooms now come equipped with them), Bible study becomes quite convenient. The bot acts as the lector for the group, looking up and presenting Scriptures on command. With a JesusFrk in the house, chatters can hold a Bible study without a "real" Bible.

Just feed the bot Scripture references, and it will provide the words from a virtual Word.

Cyberspace: Changing the Church

The presence of such online automatons raises many questions, in light of David's assertion that humans will "still be the ones who will go to church." Of course, no one who attends a Sunday morning church service or a Saturday evening mass will find an android behind the pulpit, the preacher's monotonous delivery notwithstanding. *Star Wars*-style droids are not likely to be preaching in any church house or house church anytime soon. Nevertheless, with the advent of the Internet and all of its trappings—Bible bots, hypertext online Scriptures, "streaming" video and audio of worship, and thousands of Christians assembling together in these virtual "rooms"—the church is being pressed to rethink, and perhaps expand, its definition of itself.

In today's wired world, defining *church* as merely a regular gathering of "church members" in a "church building" no longer suffices. Even before the Internet became embedded in our culture, the church had been defined more broadly. In its truest sense, the church is the company of *all* believers. It is the global church, unbound by geography or time. The Christian idea of fellowship includes the local church, but it extends beyond the local congregation to encompass believers everywhere.

Before the advent of cyberspace, this notion of a global church remained an abstraction for many of us. Even today, with the online population approaching 50 percent in the United States and Canada, few Christians recognize the Internet's potential as a medium that could broaden Christian outreach to those who might never darken a church door, foster dialogue among people of diverse faiths and denominations, and help church leaders develop a sense of unity within our diverse faith. Cloistered in our own denominations or local congregations, some of us do not see beyond the four walls of our own local fellowship, except for the occasional missionary visit and slide show.

The concept with which we're more comfortable is that of the church as a purely physical presence—a bricks-and-mortar, pews-and-pulpit church *structure*. That's the tactile church, the one we experience in our physical lives, the one we can touch. That's the church with which we're familiar: a pragmatic, experienced idea of the church as a "local" sacred assembly or congregation, a gathering of believers who join together to worship God. This physical church is an *ekklesia* (the Greek word for "assembly," from which our notion of "church" as a congregation originated).

The development of online communities of Christians, however, has made the once-abstract idea of the universal church more real, more current, more intimate. The realm of cyberspace has the potential to link the local church with the global church in new and exciting ways. An online "church" is both global and local. It is a common gathering place that transcends the boundaries of time and geography. In cyberspace, believers routinely assemble, but in a way that is foreign to our traditional idea of church. On the Internet, the church no longer requires a physical gathering. It is an *ekklesia* that encompasses the globe, a church without stained-glass windows. The online church, in the words of one observer, is a "congregation of the disembodied."[2]

Here's the Church. Where's the Steeple?

Can IRC channels such as *#ChristianTeens* be considered a true church? Do those who assemble there constitute a true *ekklesia?* Such places have no physical structure, yet they have become "places" in which Christians assemble.

Christians meet online to pray, discuss their faith, seek spiritual guidance, and study the Bible. In the language of the Internet, chat channels such as *#ChristianTeens* are "rooms." Some such rooms are even modeled after the physical church of the "real" world.[3] To the people who meet there, the chat rooms do have a sense of place. If a chat channel *is* church, it is computer-mediated church; the computer serves as the middleman. But does the fact that the adolescents who congregate on *#ChristianTeens* do so over a computer network make their experience any less legitimate than if they were to gather in a church building, in a home, or on a street corner?

For many people, this strange new world of the Internet is as real as this book that you hold in your hands. Cyberspace is rapidly becoming as transforming a force in our culture as television has been over the past half century. Teens are among the pioneers of online life. In the United States, 70 percent of all teens surf the Net, making them the most wired demographic group in the world.[4]

Moreover, this "life on the screen"[5] (to borrow Sherry Turkle's term) is influencing the spiritual lives of our children in ways that we adults might find surprising. Consider the following examples.

- An otherwise unchurched six-year-old startled his teacher (me) one Sunday morning with his response to the reading of a Scripture passage so familiar to churchgoers: *For God so loved the world, that He gave His only begotten son, that whosoever believes in Him should not perish, but have everlasting life.* "That's John verse three sixteen," the boy blurted out. (It wasn't exact chapter and verse, but it was a lot closer than some of the generally churched kids could have gotten.) "How did you know that?" I asked. "Because that's what it says on my mom's screen-saver!" he replied.
- Some 150 kids in Southampton, England, log on to Southampton's Community Church Web site (sublime .hants.org.uk) for virtual church. Although they are all members of the same local church, the kids are spread out in twenty different cell groups throughout the city, and the Web site offers them a meeting place they might not otherwise have.[6]
- Since July 1999, teens have been logging on to a Web site called the Internet Youth Group (www.geocities.com/Heartland/ Prairie/5083/) to download Bible studies and devotionals and discuss issues with other teens via the site's bulletin board.
- A three-year-old ended her bedtime recital of the Lord's Prayer with "and lead us not into temptation, but deliver us some e-mail. Amen."[7]

Touched by the Net

The preceding examples are just a few of the ways that the Internet is influencing the generation that is growing up with it. We are bombarded daily with other examples, mostly in the form of sensational media reports, that portray this new medium as something that is inherently evil and destructive to the human soul. Any form of technology undoubtedly influences behavior, and the Internet *does* pose dangers to our society. But the Internet is no more an implement of evil than is a hammer. Both objects are tools that can be used for either good or evil purposes. A Habitat for Humanity group uses hammers to build affordable homes for the needy, while vandals use them to smash car windshields. In both cases, the person, not the tool, is responsible for how the tool is used.

Will computers and the Internet ultimately contribute positively to our faith and culture? I am hopeful, but only time will tell. The Net is a young medium; whether it ends up becoming a positive influence or a detriment to our spiritual lives remains to be seen. What is certain, however, is that the Christian faith will not be left untouched by the Internet. In fact, this technology is already shaping Christianity in ways that few people in the traditional church would have imagined. Along with the rest of the Internet, the Christian presence in cyberspace has expanded tremendously over the past decade. Whereas in the mid-1990s, when the Web was just beginning to flourish, Net-surfers could find only a few hundred Christian resources on the World Wide Web, today we are awash in—some people would say flooded with—online information about our faith. The Net houses tens of thousands of Christian Web pages and thousands of Christian-oriented chat rooms, newsgroups, forums, and other online "communities." These online projects offer a wide range of services, from free electronic mail to music and movie reviews to investment advice.

The windows of cyberspace are pouring out a deluge of digital information, including the following:

- Interested in Christian music? You have thousands of Web sites from which to choose, as well as discussion groups such as *rec.music.christian* and *alt.music.christian.rock* and regularly scheduled chats with popular contemporary artists such as Jars of Clay, Audio Adrenaline, or Rebecca St. James.
- Want to study Scripture on the screen? Click on the Gospel Communication Network's Bible Gateway on the Web (bible.gospelcom.net). There you can search through nine versions of the Bible in twelve languages by typing key words or phrases into the online database. Or visit Crosswalk's Bible Study Tools (www.crosswalk.com), which offers not only Bible translations but also links to concordances, commentaries, and other study aids.
- Interested in homeschooling? Wanting to connect with other homeschoolers online? Christian-oriented Web sites abound for homeschoolers—from chat rooms for parents (www.homeschoolhaven.com) to ideas for curriculum resources (www.books4homeschool.com).

No matter what your interest is, chances are great that you'll find a resource related to it on the Internet.

Encompassing the Online World

Given the heavy interest in the Internet by ordinary Christians in the United States and elsewhere (the creators of one online survey estimate that more than one-third of Web users are Christians[8]), church leaders must recognize how ingrained this technology is becoming in the lives of their congregants and welcome the cyberchurch into the fold. The Internet is here to stay. So, too, are thousands of seekers who feel alienated from the traditional church and are turning elsewhere to find relevance, meaning, and spiritual connections.

If the church does not begin to encompass the online world in its ministry, it risks losing even more of its eroding influence in society. Although, as George Barna writes, "Americans today are more devoted to seeking spiritual enlightenment than at any previous time during the twentieth century," the church's influence in people's lives is at an all-time low. The church is not ineffectual because of its message but because "a growing majority of people have dismissed the Christian faith as weak, outdated, and irrelevant."[9] Author and pastor James Emery White concurs with Barna, noting, "People are *very* interested in spiritual things, are asking spiritual questions, and are on spiritual quests as seekers, yet they have no interest in the church."[10]

Also concurring is futurist Tom Sine. In *Mustard Seed Versus McWorld*, Sine notes that "everyone from George Gallup to *Time* magazine has documented a growing hunger for spirituality throughout the Western world,"[11] yet he laments that the church seems oblivious to this hunger and the many other challenges globalization, hastened by the Internet, is wreaking in our world. "We are living in a world changing at blinding speed," he writes, "yet in our homes, churches, and Christian colleges we unconsciously prepare our young to live and serve God in the world in which we grew up instead of in the world of the third millennium. Don't we have a responsibility to prepare our young to live in tomorrow's world?"[12]

Tomorrow's world, the wired world of instantaneous global communication, is dawning—on the Internet. The Internet poses tremendous challenges to the church, but it presents tremendous opportunity as well.

Log on for God

To reach these online seekers for God and to draw the cyberchurch into the fold, the traditional church must do the following three things.

1. We must enter the world of these cyber-seekers. We must learn about them and from them to understand how they respond to the workings of this new medium.
2. We must strive to understand the medium itself and its place and influence in our culture.

3. We must consider how we as the church should respond to the Net's growing influence in society.

This book strives to address each of the above aspects in three sections.

Part 1 discusses the characteristics of this new generation—the "N-Geners" who are staking their claim in cyberspace—and examines the challenges that these young people present to the traditional church.

Part 2 explores the online world, both the drawbacks and the benefits, to see how life on the Net affects our real-life relationships. Is the Net more akin to a sewer pipe that pumps info-sludge into our souls or a conduit for valuable information? Are people getting addicted to cyberspace? What about the dangers of cybersex and online pornography? Can computer networks actually foster a sense of community among believers?

Part 3 looks at the means and methods by which the church can respond to the pervasive and powerful influence of the online world.

Digital Discipleship

In each of these sections, the focus is on "digital discipleship," the use of the Internet as a tool to disciple young people. I neither expect nor desire the church to allow the Net to supplant more traditional methods and tools for ministry, nor do I advocate that young people abandon traditional church, Sunday school, or youth group relationships in favor of a totally virtual spiritual experience. But because we Christians are called to relate to the world in which we live, we must understand the culture and society of our times and do all that we can to influence them for Christ. As the Net becomes more influential in the lives of young people and as more children access the online world from both school and home, we Christians must be prepared to deal with the challenges that cyberspace presents. We must become salt and light in cyberspace.

Toward that goal, the end of each chapter includes a list of "*e*Connections." These Internet resources are included to help readers integrate the Internet into their ministry, their Bible study or devotional time, and their lives.

My hope is that the church will seize the power of the Net to supplement flesh-and-blood ministries. Another of my hopes is that this book will help those of us in the church who work with children, adolescents, and young adults—whether "officially" as children's ministers, youth ministers or church pastors, or unofficially as volunteers—to more fully understand the effects of the online world on those whom God has entrusted to our care. And I hope that we respond with unconditional love, which never goes out of fashion.

Finally, my hope is that we follow in cyberspace, as in all of the world, the example of Jesus Himself, who said, "Let the children come to me, and don't try to stop them!" (Matt. 19:14 CEV).

. . . .

eConnections: Online Resources for eMinistry

Religion on the Net

For an overview of the Internet's impact on religion, and vice versa, explore "Life on the Internet: Religion" (www.screen.com/start/stories/religion/default.html), the companion Web site to Discovery Canada's film documentary series, "Life on the Internet."

Virtually Sacred?

For a look at how a real-time "e-church" might function, read the paper "The Sacred and the Virtual: Religion in Multi-User Virtual Reality" (www.ascusc.org/jcmc/vol4/issue2/schroeder.html). Is the cyber-worship discussed by the authors a viable alternative to "real" church? (The paper was published in the *Journal of Computer-Mediated Communication* [www.ascusc.org/jcmc/], a resource worth bookmarking if you're interested in the way we interact via the Internet.)

Cyber Youth Group

Surf the Internet Youth Group (www.geocities.com/Heartland/ Prairie/5083/). What kinds of approaches being used on this site might be incorporated into your church's youth ministry?

Chat for Christ

If you've never experienced an online chat session, go to the ChristianChat.com Web site (www.christianchat.com) and log on to one of the many Christian chat rooms accessible through that site. What might be the benefits of such an online "church ser-vice"? What might be the drawbacks?

Network Your Ministry

Ginghamsburg Church (www.ginghamsburg.org) in Ohio, USA, has created a "cyberministry" team to broaden the church's minis-try to the online world. The ministry team also offers services to churches wanting to improve their online presence. Sign up for Ginghamsburg's CyberMinistry Forum (www.ginghamsburg.org/ cybermin/) to discuss Internet ministry with other church leaders from around the globe.

PART 1

Digital Youth

CHAPTER ONE

Wake Up! It's Time for Cyberchurch

For as the body is one, and hath many members, and all the members of that one body, being many, are one body; so also is Christ.
—1 Corinthians 12:12 KJV

The idea of seeking spiritual guidance through the Internet seems absurd to many people. But it does not seem absurd to a sixteen-year-old girl who goes by the name "LookingGlass" when she logs on to cyberspace. LookingGlass[1] attends a private Catholic high school in Louisiana. She was involved in her church when she was younger, but neither her religious education nor her earlier involvement in traditional church has done much to make her feel close to God. She describes herself as someone who drifted away from Christianity at an early age.

"As far as Church goes—I attended mostly every Friday with the school during my grammar school," she wrote in an electronic-mail note. "Now that I am in high school we have mass maybe monthly or less with the whole school. My family never really went to church accept when I was young. As I got older we made Christmas and

Easter but during my early teens we did not even do that anymore. Religion was always considered a 'personal' thing."

After grade school, she came to consider church attendance "a ritual and nothing more" and attended only when her school required it. In the summer of 1998, however, two electronic media—the radio and the Internet—converged to help bring LookingGlass closer to God.

One night I was depressed I flipped radio stations, heard a song, and started listening to Christian music. (Which is totally not anything I would have ever considered doing.) I have developed into what could be considered an underground Christian. (I don't know how it happened it was totally not my doing it is a "spirit thing" I guess.) The radio station . . . had a net page and the program, ZJAM, did too and so I began searching the net with Christian intentions. . . . Previously I did not know where to go about the faith questions I had. . . . Being able to ask questions behind a screen name allows one to get rid of the pretenses and hesitation. The Internet provides answers without human judgement and with blind encouragement (that I consider more sincere).

"I will tell you that I am about the least likely person someone would consider to go online and look up faith matters," LookingGlass continued, "but the Internet has helped me believe!!!"

The Internet provided the info on my salvation that I (was/ am) to apprehensive to get for myself in the real world. The Internet is the way to reach my generation. It is a way for cowards like me to grow in faith privately until we get the strength to say our beliefs out loud.[2]

Encouraged by the way the Internet allows her to remain anonymous in her quest for ultimate truth, LookingGlass was able to seek, and find, the answers to her questions about God, faith, and eternity. She is but one example of the "Net Generation"—young people who are turning to the Internet for spiritual guidance—and a congregant in the cyberchurch.

The Rise of the Cyberchurch

Based on a recent study of Christians and their use of the Internet, Christian sociologist George Barna predicts a "cyberchurch" emerging in the early years of the new century. Before long, Barna contends, "millions of people will never travel physically to a church, but will instead roam the Internet in search of meaningful spiritual experiences."[3]

Imagine: no more clutching a Bible as you enter your local church. No more donning your "Sunday-go-to-meeting" clothes. No more choir music. No more preaching. No hearty "amens" from fellow congregants. Instead, we'll flip a switch and commune with the Creator via our computer modems. We'll worship on the World Wide Web, log on to liturgy, and have church in a chat room.

If you find such images disturbing, you are not alone. Not many churchgoers are prepared to give up stained-glass windows for Windows 2000 and the whir of a modem. Even Christian teens—whom Barna notes are the most cybersavvy and adaptable of all believers[4]—are not ready to abandon completely their face-to-face fellowships for a virtual church. Computer-mediated discussions with several Net-savvy teens revealed that many of them are as skeptical about cyberchurch as are their elders.

"The Internet can never become to me what the church is," wrote one sixteen-year-old girl. "My faith is something that needs constant attention and you can't get that from the net."

A teenage boy concurred, writing, "I don't think the internet will ever replace conventional church for the majority of people."

Similarly, twenty-year-old Melanie, a student at the University of Portland, added, "Talking with people on the Internet about Christ and all is great, but nothing could really take the place of someone being there in person to talk to and to pray with."

Online chatters or e-mail pen pals "cannot hug you," wrote a nineteen-year-old student at the University of Wisconsin, "and there is no accountability on the net because these people cannot see you in your daily life."[5]

Such comments might come as no surprise if they were originating on the keyboards of older adults or others who are not so immersed in the digital culture. The irony of these statements, however, is that they come from young people who spend significantly more time—some as much as twenty hours a week—discussing matters of faith on the Net than even the most devout Christian normally spends with traditional church activities. Two young men in this discussion group, who are from different continents, spend hours each week collaborating on their Christian music electronic magazine (e-zine), while a sixteen-year-old from Salem, Oregon, designs Web sites for independent Christian rock groups. One college student on the list maintains a Web site that promotes some four hundred Christian bands, while another takes part in an online community for Christian writers.

The Cyberchurch Is Here

Despite the skepticism of this group of teens and twenty-somethings, plenty of evidence exists that the online church is already here, and it is growing dramatically. And young people are leading the way in this new expression of the faith. Dawson McAllister, a veteran youth minister, notes that "Millions of young people soar through cyberspace to exchange experiences on personal computers, and pace cars on the information superhighway are driven by teenagers." In addition, the Internet revolution "has brought them more fully into the global society and given them a larger share of the perils and pleasures of their time."[6]

While many media reports focus on the perils of cyberspace, many teens find the Internet to be a positive force in their lives. A 1999 survey of Christian teens who use the Internet found that the majority of them feel freer to discuss their faith over the Net than in face-to-face conversations. Contrary to the belief that the Internet draws people away from traditional institutions such as church and family, most of these teens said that they were just as involved in church activities today as they were before getting on the Net. In some instances, the teens were even more active in church since they logged onto cyberspace.[7]

Some young Christians have discovered that the Net is teeming with opportunities to share Christ. Among them is the teenager who posted the following encouraging message on one of the "Live the Life Online" forums sponsored by the DC/LA youth evangelism organization.

> I was writing to a friend over email, but I had never met him, I was just introduced to him by a friend. I wrote to him for a while and he was really nice, but he was always really depressed. I always tried to encourage him. Then one day, he wrote to me telling me that his life was over, and that he was going to slit his wrists, mutilate his body and then kill himself. I was really scared, but I didn't know where he lived, or how I could help him. I told my parents, but they didn't know what to do either. So I sat down with my Bible, and wrote to him. I told him about how he could get saved, and how God loves him. Amazingly enough, he listened. . . . Later on in the week, he asked me about some other things about God. I don't think he is saved yet, but he is still asking questions.[8]

From Virtual Soda Shop to Spiritual Mall

Cyberspace is quickly becoming the hangout of choice for young people. For many cybersavvy teens, the Internet is the first "place" they go when they get home from school.[9] Several ministries are taking note of the power of cyberspace, particularly its ability to reach young people who, like LookingGlass, have become alienated from traditional religious institutions. Campus Crusade for Christ International, a parachurch organization that is well known for reaching young people with the gospel, reports that 40 percent of its Web site's visitors are younger than twenty-five years of age.[10]

And ministries such as the Billy Graham Evangelistic Association are harnessing the Net's power to get young people away from their keyboards and to their crusades. In 1997, the ministry launched an online ad campaign to attract Net-surfers to crusades in the San Francisco area. Playing on a well-known Microsoft slogan, the association's Web-based ads asked surfers, "Where do you want to go tomorrow?" Echoing George Barna's sentiments, the crusade's director, Rick Marshall, explains the reason for the online approach: "The audience is out of the church and they're not coming back, but they're still on a search."[11]

Much of that searching occurs online. Even members of the body of Christ are turning to the Net for answers. Christians are online in big numbers; they comprise 38.4 percent of the Internet population, according to one survey.[12] Millions of Christians enter cyberspace daily to enrich their spiritual lives through virtual prayer, worship, and evangelism. Perhaps these activities don't seem like "real church" to many believers, including those who routinely practice their faith online. Perhaps, too, few people in the traditional church recognize the influence that cyberspace exerts on the faithful, and vice versa. Nevertheless, the fact remains that the Net is an important part of many Christians' lives, and its influence in our lives is growing daily.

People from all walks of life continue to seek spiritual guidance, but fewer people are looking to the church for answers. All too often, they see the church as increasingly irrelevant. Jimmy Long, in his book *Generating Hope,* writes, "The unchanging church will be unable to draw in new members and will continue to lose its youth, who feel the church has no answers for their struggles. The result for many of these churches will be extinction by the time the emerging postmodern generation comes into maturity."[13]

According to George Barna's research, one out of every six churchgoing teenagers expects to rely increasingly on the Internet to meet their spiritual needs in the coming years. These Christian teens will be part of a significant portion of the U.S. population— up to one-fifth, Barna predicts—who will rely entirely on the Internet for their religious needs.[14]

From Unchurched to Cyberchurched?

This gravitation to the Net is part of a larger phenomenon saddling the modern church: the growing number of "unchurched" Americans, a group that includes many former churchgoers and many people who consider themselves Christians but see no need for regular fellowship within traditional church settings. Barna predicts that "within the next fifteen years a majority of Americans will be completely isolated from the traditional church format." This group includes a significant number of Christians who will have decided that the traditional church does not meet their needs. Many of them will be in cell groups and home churches, others will be unchurched, and still others will be venturing out into cyberspace, as congregants of the cyberchurch.[15]

Given these trends, debating whether an online church is a "true" church is not nearly as important as is formulating a response to the sweeping cultural changes that are diminishing the church's influence. The real issue for the church as we contemplate the virtual mission field of the Internet is how we will respond. Will the church be there for online seekers with a message of salvation and hope? Or will we choose instead to ignore the impact of this new medium and let other belief systems influence the hearts and minds of Net surfers? Will we choose to offer a Christ-centered alternative to the growing influences of New Age religions, shoot-'em-up cybergames, and virtual sex parlors? Or will we choose instead to lash out against the evils of cyberspace, railing against the dangers of online pornography, multiuser virtual games, and cybersex without offering an alternative, thereby further alienating the online community?

Unfortunately, the church's track record of responding to the threats of new media is not good. Whenever new challenges to the faith arise, the church tends to respond inappropriately. All too often, modern congregations either stick their heads in the sand, ignoring the changes sweeping through the larger culture, or they become reactionary, further alienating those whom they should be reaching. As author and minister David Fisher explains in his book

The 21st Century Pastor, "Some churches deny reality and continue business as usual. Failing to understand the times, they just keep talking to themselves and, consequently, make less and less of a dent in their world." Other churches "curse the moral and spiritual failure of our time and work furiously to turn back the tide of time. But the sheer numbers of non-Christian people, along with the pluralist and tolerant mood of the times, seem to make that a futile battle."[16]

Jimmy Long echoes Fisher's sentiments. "As we move into the twenty-first century many Christians continue to minister as if they were living in the nineteenth century, convinced that they are merely ministering as Jesus did in the first century. God calls us to be like the 'men of Issachar, who understood the times and knew what Israel should do' [1 Chron. 12:32 NIV]."[17]

Today, the church—*all* Christians—must recognize that the Internet is a valuable tool to reach the generations. The church must take advantage of all that the Net has to offer—much as it has effectively used, and continues to use, broadcast and print media to share the gospel message. But the church also must recognize that the Internet is more than a mere tool or technology. It also encompasses a "world"—an entirely new culture—into which the church must enter if it is to fulfill the Great Commission. The Net, then, is both a tool (a medium through which further to share the good news) and a mission field (a world populated by people who desperately need to hear our message).

Six Characteristics of the Cyberchurch

George Barna is right: the cyberchurch is coming. But what will this cyberchurch look like, and will we recognize it when we see it?

The pace of technological change on the Internet is so mind-bending that I would not dare to speculate what the Netchurch of five years from now, or even one year from now, will look like. But I do think that the Internet—both the medium and the online culture—is forcing those ministries that are already online to think about—and do—ministry differently. I see six characteristics that are transforming Internet ministries. To be successful on the

Internet, at least during these formative years of Net culture, a ministry must assume these characteristics.

Interactive, Not Passive

"The institutional church has always had a stake in promoting passivity," wrote Robert Wuthnow long before the Internet became a household word. "Preachers who fill live pulpits generally find their burdens easier if their parishioners sit quietly and listen, responding only when the choirmaster directs or when the plate is passed."[18] Such passivity is anathema on the Net. This is an interactive medium, one that encourages, and in some cases requires, involvement.

Interactivity, writes media critic Jon Katz, "is critically important to the young, who have little experience with passive media. From Nintendo to cable channels to zapper-controlled TVs and computers, the young are accustomed to varying degrees of choice in all their media."[19] Whether young or old, online congregants won't stand for the type of passivity that is so prevalent in the institutional church. Written Web page "sermons" incorporate hypertext links to Scripture, visuals, audio clips, and other online resources to appeal to an online congregation that expects to be involved and engaged by the Net ministry. Chat room Bible discussions are much more interactive and engaging than the typical church Bible study. Aida Sultanyan, who engages in virtual Bible studies at Christianity Today's women's area (www.christianitytoday.com), points out the benefits of such online communication: "In a real-life Bible study, when you're in a room full of women, people are afraid to open up. You cannot be as transparent as you ought to be. But online, because it's anonymous, women feel free to open and say what they need to say. People are honest, and there's confession."[20]

Networked, Not Hierarchical

The Net is the most antihierarchical communications medium ever devised. It facilitates the free flow of information, often to the detriment of institutions that are more interested in stifling that flow than in facilitating it. Institutions that try to control the flow of information on the Net through traditional organizational structures will be seen as ineffective, and they won't succeed in cyberspace.

The Worldwide Church of God learned this hard lesson in 1995. Best known for the end-times eschatology of its flamboyant founder, Herbert W. Armstrong, and the magazine he founded, *The Plain Truth,* the Worldwide Church of God began changing some of its doctrinal stances after Armstrong's death in 1986. When the church leadership announced some significant changes in 1995, many of the church's most ardent followers began debating these changes via Internet forums. This grassroots online movement challenged the organization's top-down communications structure. The Internet nearly broke the hierarchy of the Worldwide Church of God.[21]

Cyberspace, as Jeff Zaleski explains in *The Soul of Cyberspace,* "will favor those religions and spiritual teachings that tend toward anarchy and that lack a complex hierarchy."[22] Indeed, many of the most successful Net ministries are anything but traditional. Several of them are low-budget Web outreaches birthed of the desires of a single person or a small group to share the gospel with the online audience. But whether big or small, shoestring or big-budget, ministries must learn to adapt to the loosely structured world of cyberspace.

One of the more structured organizations that has made a name for itself on the Net is the Gospel Communications Network (www.gospelcom.net). This evangelical ministry has taken advantage of the online world's networked environment, creating a hypertext Bible in several versions and languages and collaborating with hundreds of other ministries, large and small alike. As a result, the Gospel Communications Network generates more online activity than any other single Christian Web site today. It is the only Christian ministry to rank consistently in the top five hundred most visited Web sites.[23] In a sense, it is the online world's first true megaministry.

Postmodern, Not Modern

We live in an era when the notion of objective truth is under attack from all sides. The traditional custodians of rational and objective "truth"—the church, modern science, the university, the democratic model of government—have fallen from their high places. Now, truth is in the eye of the beholder, and "choice" has become the supreme virtue in a society of shoppers. This is a symptom of our culture's shift from *modernism*—the philosophy born of the Enlightenment, when reason and empiricism became the basis for judging all truth—to *postmodernism*. (This shift will be discussed in more detail in chapter four.) The Net is a medium that is well suited for these postmodern times. It is a great leveler, putting all religions, regardless of their credibility, on equal footing. Christianity competes with New Age and pagan belief systems to be heard in this global marketplace. To be effective in this postmodern environment, Christian ministries must face the fact that our faith is no longer seen as "the way, the truth, and the life" (John 14:6 KJV), but as merely one of many possible "true" religions. The days of Christianity's privileged standing in society have passed. The church must present its traditional truths to a congregation that is accepting of a variety of religious truths and perspectives, many of them anything but traditional.

Questioning, Not Accepting

In keeping with this postmodern ideology that rejects objective truth, the congregants of cyberchurch will be even more likely to question the authority of the institutional church than their skeptical baby boomer elders. This questioning will empower more believers to take an active role in shaping church reforms. The successful cyberchurch will not only welcome questioning and inquiry from the faithful but also encourage participants to probe beyond the surface of traditional Christian faith to deepen their beliefs. Credible cyberministries will provide online resources for inquisitive cybersaints.

Collaborative, Not Isolationist

In cyberspace, denominational distinctions become blurred. At first glance, the differences matter little to the postmodern Internet surfer. "Like the Berlin Wall, the barriers between Christian groups that once seemed so impassable now suddenly appear ready for demolition," explains writing consultant Eric Stanford. "The fundamental idea behind this is that our ultimate commitment should be to Christ and to his church (universally conceived) rather than to any cultural entity set up at some point in history."[24] Consequently, the successful cyberchurch will seek to collaborate and cooperate with other online ministries.

The Gospel Communications Network and Leadership University (www.leaderu.com) stand out as models of collaboration for traditional ministries and parachurch organizations to emulate. Also, individuals, small groups, and even local churches in a community can come together online to provide a united, collaborative front to Net culture. Some Net-based ministries will succeed by enlisting the help of people from distant lands. An evangelical Web ministry called "A Voice in the Wilderness" (www.fishthe.net/avitw) was created through just such an international collaboration. Christians in England, Denmark, and the United States worked together to develop this online outreach to non-Christians. Although some of the team members have never met face-to-face, they have nevertheless launched an effective cyberministry and resource for people who are interested in Internet evangelism.

Asynchronous, Not Time Bound

The online church is unfettered by time or space. At any time and across the time zones, two or more Christians can gather in Christ's name in a chat room and "have church." One participant might be in his pajamas and munching on a breakfast bagel while the other, several time zones away, might be logging on at the end of a long day. With the Net, it doesn't matter. The boundaries of time and space are transcended. Church on the Net is not a weekly or twice-weekly occurrence. Church can occur at any time and at any place.

While each of these characteristics presents new challenges to the traditional church and to individual Christians who are intent on entering the world of the Internet, the biggest challenge to the church is the Internet generation itself.

. . . .

eConnections: Online Resources for eMinistry

Z-Jammin' for God
🏹

Check out the ZJAM Youth Ministries Web site (www.zjam .com)—the same site that helped LookingGlass discover the Christian faith. Why might such a site be more appealing to a teen than a more traditional church Web site?

Getting into Their Heads
🏹

How well do teens get along with their parents? What issues do teens worry about the most? What influences how they think and act? Answers to these and other mysteries can be found in a recent *Group* magazine survey of Christian teenagers (www.groupmag.com/ survey/default.htm).

Youth Stats, Part One
🏹

Barna Research Online (www.barna.org) provides timely demographic research into the state of the church in the USA. Ponder the statistics about teenagers or read about the future "cyberchurch."

Youth Stats, Part Two
🏹

For a glimpse into how teens are using the Net, read the report "Youth: Next on the Net" from TheStandard.com (www.thestandard. com), the companion Web site to *The Industry Standard* magazine.

Virtual Teachings for Youth Pastors

Youth evangelist Winkie Pratney's Virtual Classroom for Youth Pastors (www.gospelcom.net/moh/WinkPrat/RA/VirtualClassroom .htm) provides some excellent audio and video teachings from this veteran minister. Gain insight into the Net Generation by taking in the audio lesson "Digital Generation," then check out the video study titled "Paul and the X-Files."

CHAPTER TWO

Meet the Net Generation

*One generation passeth away, and another generation
cometh.*

—*Ecclesiastes 1:4* KJV

BEHOLD THE CLASS OF 2001.

Here they come, nearly 3 million strong,[1] high school diplomas
in hand, ready to take on the world.

Most of them have never used a rotary-dial telephone or wound
a wristwatch, yet they can create their own CDs with music they
download from the Internet.

They've never played Pac-Man, Space Invaders, or any other
two-dimensional video arcade game. Yet they navigate with ease
through the adventurous 3-D computer worlds of Lara Croft, Crash
Bandicoot, and Duke Nukem.

They've never had to get off the couch to change television channels. Remote controls have been around for as long as they can
remember.

Chances are, they've never played a vinyl record; the compact
disc was born before they were.

They know nothing of an exploding space shuttle, the Chernobyl nuclear disaster, or the Tiananmen Square uprising. The Persian Gulf War is a fading memory.

They have never known two Germanies or more than one pope.

They have never known a world without AIDS or ESPN.

They are the first generation to be born into Luvs, Huggies, and Pampers.

The names John, Paul, George, and Ringo mean nothing to them, but Sporty, Scary, Baby, Ginger, and Posh do.

The "Peanuts" gang—Charlie Brown, Snoopy, Lucy, Linus, and Pigpen—has been replaced by the foul-mouthed "South Park" kids—Stan, Kyle, Cartman, and Kenny.

To them, U2 is a rock band, not a reconnaissance plane.

They recognize Austin 3:16 but not John 3:16.

They have spent more than half of their lives with Bart Simpson.

They grew up with Microsoft, IBM PCs, in-line skates, and NutraSweet.[2]

And they are the future of the church.

Talkin' 'bout Their Generation

Just as the church was beginning to understand Generation X— that demographic cohort of skeptical, alienated kids that came along after the baby boomers—along comes a new group of young people to be figured out. The Class of 2001 represents a wave crest of this new generation, a generation that is poised to crash into our culture like a tsunami. Sometimes called Generation Y, the Millennials, Mosaics, or the "echo boom," the oldest members of this group were born in the late seventies, sandwiched between the demise of disco and the rise of Ronald Reagan's "morning in America." This generation bridges the centuries, spanning into the early years of the new millennium. Today, the oldest members of this generation are now in their early twenties, and the youngest members are in diapers.

Already, certain characteristics are distinguishing this generation from its predecessors. Just as Generation X was characterized—and often stereotyped—as an alienated, angst-ridden, distrustful generation, so this new group of youngsters will become known as a generation with its own unique distinguishing features.

What makes this generation different? Several things. Among the most notable difference is the rise of the Internet and its influence in their lives. Don Tapscott, the author of *Growing Up Digital: The Rise of the Net Generation,* sees the Net as the major force shaping this generation's character. The Net is so central to these youngsters' lives, Tapscott claims, that he has coined the term "the Net Generation" to describe them.

This is the first generation to grow up in a truly digital age. Television was the technology that defined the baby boomers. Generation X grew up with television, Walkmans, and Gameboys. But just as those technologies helped to define the boomers and the Xers, the computer and the Internet defines "N-Geners."[3]

At Home on the Net

"For the first time in history," Tapscott writes, "children are more comfortable, knowledgeable, and literate than their parents about an innovation central to society. And it is through the use of the digital media that the N-Generation will develop and superimpose its culture on the rest of society."[4] This "generation lap" means a role reversal for many families. No longer are the elders the keepers of the wisdom. Rick and Kathy Hicks write, "Our children are lapping us in their knowledge of computers and the digital revolution. They navigate on the Internet almost by instinct, while we struggle to understand how it all works and how to get what we want."[5] Writing in *Christianity Today,* Wendy Murray Zoba notes that these kids are "the most plugged-in generation ever" and that their electronic sphere, including cyberspace, "has become their community, their tribe, their family."[6]

They are at home in this nascent digital age. In the words of one of their own, fourteen-year-old Neasa Coll, "Kids today are growing up with the Internet, and the Internet is growing up with kids."[7] Microsoft cofounder Bill Gates has affixed another label on a subset of this new generation. Gates is calling those youngsters who were born since 1994 "Generation I" because they will never know life without the Internet. They will grow up "in a world where everything is online, and that will be taken for granted."[8]

And so we see the generation lap demonstrated in traditional media, such as with the Ameritrade television commercial in which Stewart, a whiz kid with multicolored hair, teaches his boss, a corporate suit named "Mr. Big," how to use the Net to trade stocks. "Ride the wave of the future, my man," Stewart tells his boss, just before inviting him to a weekend party.

Shiny, Happy People?

Much of the popular writing about the Net Generation exudes optimism—in stark contrast to the popular descriptions of their predecessors, Generation X. Newspaper reports describe this young generation as optimistic, moral, and entrepreneurial.[9] Trend-spotters Janine Lopiano-Misdom and Joanne De Luca have called today's youth culture "the most resourceful, intellectual, and creative generation that we have seen in the past fifty years."[10] Demographers William Strauss and Neil Howe describe "the vanguard" of this generation as "cute," "cheerful," "scoutlike" and "wanted,"[11] adding that the kids are "riding a powerful crest of protective concern, dating back to the early 1980s, over the American childhood environment."[12]

But things aren't always as rosy for N-Geners as some writers describe. Many of the problems that plagued Generation X, such as high divorce rates, teenage crime and drug use, teen pregnancies, and the high percentage of children in poverty, haven't disappeared altogether. Some conditions, such as the poverty rate among children, have worsened in recent years. A November 1999 report titled "Ten Critical Threats to America's Children: Warning Signs for the Next Millennium" pointed out that one of every five kids in the United States lives in poverty, that 11.1 million children under the age of eighteen have no health insurance, and that each year 3 million teens contract AIDS, HIV, or other sexually transmitted diseases.[13] Moreover, even while Strauss and Howe write glowingly of this generation, others paint a different picture of today's youth. Not all N-Geners are happy campers.

In her book *A Tribe Apart: A Journey into the Heart of American Adolescence,* Patricia Hersch describes the struggles of fourteen-year-old Brendon, an N-Gener whose brooding nature evokes the characteristics of the previous generation. Like many teens today, Brendon has a keen interest in spiritual matters. He "spends long hours discussing God and faith with his sister," Hersch writes, but he "doesn't feel the same way about God as she does. He feels like God has let him down. 'What good is a God that you can't come to terms with in your own way, and you have to follow some set of rules?' he wonders."[14]

The Net can contribute to the sense of pessimism among today's youngsters. "Kids can see anything on the Net," says DeeDee Gordon, director of market research for Lambesis, Inc., of Del Mar, California. "You hear that a lot, but think about it: They can see violence and destruction. They can learn about sleazy political officials. They can view autopsy pictures. As a result, they're much more pessimistic than adults."[15]

Defining the Net Generation

Like all previous generations, N-Geners are a mixed bag. There are the brooding Brendons and the pessimistic Netheads as well as the "scoutlike" kids that Strauss and Howe describe. But as with every other demographic group that sociologists study, the Net Generation possesses certain characteristics worth observing if we are to gain a better understanding of how they think, how they act, how they are motivated, and how they relate to spiritual matters.

One of the most significant characteristics is this generation's sheer numbers. Already the N-Geners have eclipsed the boomers in population, and they are fast becoming a force with which marketers, educators, and the church must reckon. The United States alone has 81.1 million N-Geners, or 30 percent of the nation's population. Baby boomers, whom we've come to think of as the biggest population group our society has ever seen, amount to *only* 77.2 million, now 29 percent of the U.S. population.[16]

Despite the numbers, the new generation has yet to flex its collective muscle. But when it does, watch out. Soon N-Geners will push their boomer predecessors off center-stage in the realm of popular culture. This new generation "will be detonated by the kids who were born during the baby boomlet of 1989 to 1994," writes journalist Nathan Cobb.[17] During that time, more than four million babies were born in the United States annually. Kids born during that period are now in grade schools and middle schools. The real number crunch will hit in 2007, when members of that boomlet are high school students. In 2007, two million more kids will be in high school than there were in 1997, and some 451,000 high school graduates "will be bound for somewhere."[18]

These numbers alone present a remarkable challenge to the church. Are our nation's churches equipped to accommodate a sudden influx of children and young adults? More important, are we aware of the cultural forces that are influencing the way this generation thinks or the way they make decisions and receive information?

The Net Generation brings with it much more than the sheer numbers. These kids present many other issues with which the church is ill-prepared to deal. Among the most critical issues are the following.

They Come from Disintegrating Families

The trend toward single-parent households, which turned many Xers into "latchkey kids" in the eighties, has exploded with the Net Generation. Single-parent households are becoming the norm. Between one-quarter and one-third of kids born between 1989 and 1994 were born to unmarried women. This trend is changing the way people, especially children, think about family life. A 1997 study found that four of five children between the ages of nine and seventeen consider a one-parent home normal.[19] Churches that build ministries on the assumption that two-parent households are the norm will need to change their approaches to ministry.

They Are Multicultural

The Net Generation is "the most racially blended, borderless generation we have ever seen."[20] About three-fourths of today's children and teens have friends who are of a different ethnic origin.[21] As a result, N-Geners are generally more tolerant of racial and ethnic differences than are their predecessors. This fact likely will lead to a greater tolerance of non-Christian belief systems, as N-Geners "draw from a deeper crosscurrent of cultures" than did young people from previous generations.[22] More young people will be of mixed race, further blurring racial boundaries. The Net will facilitate this trend toward multiculturalism and tolerance, providing N-Geners with more information about different cultures, societies, races, and religions from all over the world.

Tapscott sees this as a positive trend. Because of this greater tolerance and openness to differences, says Tapscott, the Net Generation "may be more colorblind and oblivious to gender and other social differences than any other culture in history."[23] He quotes sixteen-year-old Lauren Verity: "Race, color, religion—none of this matters on the Internet. It doesn't have to exist, and most of us don't care anyway."[24]

Veteran youth minister Dawson McAllister sees reason to be concerned about today's "passionately tolerant" teens. Describing this generation as "spiritual, but without focus," McAllister notes that N-Geners are "very God-conscious" but not grounded in the Christian faith; "they don't know which god to pursue."[25] In the face of this multicultural generation, churches must present the truth of the Christian message while understanding the "crosscurrent of cultures" from which young people will draw their ideas.

They Are Postmodern

Just as N-Geners are the first to grow up in a truly digital world, they also are the first purely "postmodern" generation. Postmodernism, which is discussed further in chapter 4, is a worldview that tends to reject the idea of objective truth. This tendency

presents the church with unique challenges. "Postmodern think-
ers claim that any attempt to make everyone accept the same truth
is an insult to their cultural identity," writes Dennis McCallum,
the author of *The Death of Truth*. According to postmodern reasoning, "Instead of trying to make everyone agree with our view,
we should celebrate diversity—that is, we should accept and 'respect' others' realities and others' truths."[26]

This postmodern philosophy stems in part from the multiculturalism of N-Gen culture. It also relates to the influences of
computers and the Net. Tapscott characterizes N-Geners as "young
navigators"[27]—a theme that is common in the postmodern philosophy, which maintains that truth can be attained only by ex-
ploration, experience, and self-discovery. The challenge for the
church is to make Christianity relevant in this postmodern world
of relative truth.

They Live by the Consumption Ethic

Film critic David Denby's teenage son hits the computer first
thing in the morning before breakfast, and Denby worries that his
son's generation is being shaped into consumers "before they've had
a chance to develop their souls."[28] The consumerism ethic that is so
rampant in today's world is an outgrowth of the postmodernist philosophy, which touts choice and diversity as supreme virtues. Os
Guinness describes life in the postmodern world as "shopping-mall
or catalogue consumerism, allowing us to buy our way to a connois-
seurship of surface and style. We pick out the bits and pieces of our
consumer choice and assemble them into our own versions of who
we are and how we live."[29]

This consumerism extends into the realm of spirituality, where
the sacred is packaged and marketed as "just another product in
the broader marketplace of goods and services."[30] The church itself "is often seen as a place to receive goods and services rather
than as a body whose purpose it is to serve," notes one commenta-
tor,[31] as "The people with whom we desire to share the gospel have
become reluctant buyers of the faith, guarded shoppers casually

browsing through the religious options in search of something that fits."[32] N-Geners inherited their consumerist ethic from their baby boomer parents. As a *USA Today* article explains, "From Barbie to rock 'n' roll to low-fat diets, baby boomers have been dictating popular culture for decades. Now their influence as the nation's dominant marketing force is about to be superseded by their kids."[33] Today, says media critic Douglas Rushkoff, "our new religion is to become more plugged-in, in whatever way possible, to the way the world works. The purpose of life is to buy and sell things, or even ideas," and "our ruthless commerce is no longer limited to products but now includes lifestyles, political candidates, morality, and even religions."[34]

N-Geners are already church shopping, choosing their own places of worship rather than following their parents to church.[35] Other teens aren't as likely to shop for a church as they are for a customized belief system that "works" for them. As Harvard University theologian Harvey Cox explains, young people "want to pick and choose and are less willing to accept religions either as full-blown systems of truth or as authoritative institutions."[36] The church must resist the urge to placate N-Gen "shoppers" by offering them a menu of services that water down the mission and message of Christianity. "The church," Os Guinness writes, "cannot become simply another customer center that offers designer religion and catalogue spirituality to the hoppers and shoppers of the modern world."[37]

They're on the Net

At the moment, N-Geners are relatively few. But their numbers will mushroom as the Net becomes more prominent among families in the coming years. According to a report from Jupiter Communications, only about 10 percent of kids between the ages of two and seventeen had Net access in their homes in 1997, but by 2002 about half of America's teens will be logging on to the Net from home.[38] A 1999 report from Arbitron NewMedia says that already about 62 percent of kids between the ages of eight and fifteen use the Web.[39]

And that's in just the United States. Globally, Net usage is expected to more than double, from 349 million in 2000 to 766 million by 2005. The World Wide Web will live up to its name, with one-third of all Internet connections being in eastern and western Europe and one-fourth being in the Pacific Rim countries of Asia.[40]

The Net will soon be as prevalent in homes as television and the telephone, and this fact is bound to influence the way N-Geners think and relate to their world. Writer Nathan Cobb notes that "the decentralized and two-way Internet clearly changes the way many kids get information. It alters how they build friendships. It gives them a global orientation. And it offers them speed."[41] Making the church relevant to the Net Generation will involve a thorough understanding of this preferred method of communication.

They Need a Cause

Despite the optimism that Tapscott, Strauss and Howe, and other observers express about this generation, many people see a void in the N-Gener soul that only God can fill. Youth minister Dawson McAllister finds this emptiness among the teens he encounters in his many youth crusades. "Recently," he writes, "I asked students to identify the causes of their generation, and blank expressions were their answers."[42]

Likewise, Christian writer Wendy Murray Zoba also senses despair and apathy among this generation. Her profile of the Class of 2000 for *Christianity Today* reveals the need for these teens to become engaged in something bigger than themselves. "My generation seems oblivious," says one teen quoted in Zoba's article. "We don't do anything; we don't have any great achievements," says another. Yet another says, "We feel like everything is changing and we have nothing to do with it, so we sit back and let it happen." "We have nothing to grasp; no one to look up to; no one to believe in." "We're just coasting." "We're not standing for anything." "We desperately need to be standing for something."[43]

What will be the church's response to this plea for meaning?

Will we offer them something with which to identify? Will we present them with a cause?

As we look at these demographic characteristics, it's important that we also examine this new generation in light of other generations. How do these kids differ from their predecessors, especially in terms of their approach to spirituality and to life on the Internet? That is the subject of the next chapter.

. . . .

eConnections: Online Resources for eMinistry

Instructions Not Required

In a newspaper interview (archived online at web.mit.edu/sturkle/www/bosglobe.html), cyberspace sociologist Sherry Turkle notes that N-Geners don't need to "read the instructions" before immersing themselves in the technological toys at their disposal. When it comes to technology, today's teens, tweens, and children are improvisational whiz kids. "With the Furby, children don't read the instructions," Turkle says. "They just pick it up and start playing. The computer culture rewards this type of tinkering, this type of cognitive risk-taking. I call it the triumph of tinkering." How might this "tinkering" carry over into how the Net Generation approaches traditional Christianity? What about other forms of spirituality?

Virtual da Vincis?

Swanky (swanky.org) is a Net hangout for N-Geners with an artistic flair—those who create with Photoshop and html on a canvas of digital space. Visit the site to get a feel for what young artists are saying about their new medium.

Christian Teens

Part of the About.com online universe, the Christian Teens Web community (christianteens.about.com) is a popular hangout for, well, Christian teens. But non-Christian teens also visit the site to discuss spiritual issues in the site's forum and chat room. What is it about the site that makes it so appealing to Christians and non-Christians alike?

Teens on a Mission

Teen Mania Ministries (www.teenmania.org) not only sends N-Geners on short-term mission trips but also provides a forum through which these "Maniacs" can strengthen their newfound friendships online.

CHAPTER THREE

Boomer, Xer, N-Gener

Come now, and let us reason together.
                    —*Isaiah 1:18* KJV

THE IRC CHANNEL *#Christian* welcomes believers of all ages and denominations. Teens, twentysomethings, and older chat enthusiasts frequent the channel, making it a good stop in cyberspace for someone who wants to get a sense of how the online faithful share their ideas. So one evening in the summer of 1998, I popped in to conduct one of the many informal surveys that form a good part of this book's research.

"I have a question for the teens in this room," I typed. "I've been reading a lot about the 'cyberchurch' lately, and I wonder how many teens here would prefer to meet in cyberspace instead of attend a youth group meeting in a traditional church setting."

It got quiet for a moment. ("Quiet" in chat room parlance means no typed text scrolls by on the screen.) Then one of the forum's elders, a fortysomething named Dave, responded.

"Never forsake the assembling together of yourselves, in church," Dave typed, quoting a fragment of Hebrews 10:25 but adding two little words—*in church*—to shade the meaning of that Scripture.

That got the ball rolling. A twentysomething who used the

nickname Eirene quickly challenged, "Where in the Bible does Jesus say to build a church to worship together in?" A couple of others in Eirene's age group chimed in. "Actually, Jesus teaches that we will worship Him in our hearts, as opposed to the tabernacles," wrote one. "In Hebrews we are called together as an assembly. The physical building is irrelevant."

Then a teenage girl chimed in. "I don't think it matters where you are or who you are with," she said in her text message to the channel. "If you are worshiping God, then you are worshiping God."

So began this impromptu theological exchange among #Christian's volunteer spokespeople for the three predominant generations of our day: the boomers, Generation X, and the emerging Net Generation. In their brief responses, each chatter managed to capture the essence of his or her generation, and the statements of each prove very insightful.

The first to respond was Dave, the baby boomer and channel "elder," who emphasized the importance of a physical church structure in worship. Next came Eirene, the Xer, who quickly questioned Dave's authority and his idea of Christian worship. Finally, the teenage girl spoke, saying that it did not matter whether churchgoers gathered in a building or online, typifying her generation's ambiguity and flexibility toward ideas that previous generations hold as definite.

The three generations represented by these respondents constitute the majority of Net users today. (Net demographics are changing rapidly, however. Preschoolers and octogenarians alike are logging on with equal enthusiasm, and the fastest growing segment of Net users is women over the age of fifty.)[1] Although the Net Generation is the focus of this book, it is impossible to understand the N-Geners without first examining previous generations and comparing their traits with today's young people. N-Geners are in large part the legacy of boomers and Xers, but they also differ to the extent that we must learn about the "other" to understand better just how these N-Geners are coming into their own.

Any attempt to describe a generation in a mere few pages will undoubtedly gloss over several important elements of that group.

In addition, there are always exceptions to any generational characterization. Not every baby boomer was idealistic in his or her youth, nor are all members of Generation X slackers or born cynics. The following descriptions of each group, however, are generalities that seem to typify a large portion of each generation.[2]

The Baby Boomers

Dave's generation is the much-analyzed post-World War II group known as the baby boomers. The idealists of the sixties and seventies, who marched for civil rights and against the Vietnam War, are now entering middle age. The ones who coined the phrase "don't trust anyone over thirty" continue to cling to the youth culture they helped create, even as more of them become eligible for AARP cards. In their youth, many boomers invigorated mainstream Christianity with their idealism, seeking to make God more relevant to their lives. Boomers led the "Jesus movement" of the late sixties and early seventies and built the "seeker-sensitive" churches of the seventies and early eighties. Organizations such as Jesus People USA, headquartered in downtown Chicago, and the Willow Creek Community Church, in Chicago's suburbs, both stand today as monuments to the baby boomers' movements to enliven the American church.

This generation came of age during a time of great social unrest, with the civil rights and antiwar movements galvanizing them to question authority, take a stand against racial intolerance, and protest America's military involvement in Vietnam. At the same time, many boomers turned away from Christianity, which had come to represent the "establishment" against which they rebelled. Some of them became disillusioned by the church's apathy toward racism and the Vietnam War, whereas others decided to explore alternative religions as influential rock groups such as the Beatles, the Grateful Dead, and others popularized non-Christian worldviews with their music and lifestyles. The drug and rock cultures intertwined, and young people in the sixties experimented with drugs more openly than had any other generation before them. Another drug, the birth-control pill, "liberated" boomers to experiment sexually without concern for the consequences. For the most hedonistic of boomers, "sex, drugs and rock 'n' roll" was the prevailing mind-set.

Many of the same spiritual attitudes that gained clout and popularity in the sixties later influenced the broader world of business and popular culture. The generation that challenged our values in the sixties are now defining society's values at the turn of the millennium. Today, boomers such as Bill Gates, the cofounder of Microsoft; Steve Jobs of Apple Computers; and Mitch Kapor, who created the software company Lotus, have not only set the tone for the computer industry but also shaped the mores of our networked society. Gates has gone on to build Microsoft into a multinational corporate giant, the proverbial eight-hundred-pound gorilla that sets the tenor for computer and Internet culture. The modeling of Microsoft's ubiquitous Windows operating platform as an "office," with the screen as a "desktop" and computer data organized into "files," says a lot about the corporate ethos influencing our identities on the screen.[3] More so than the family, the community, or the church, the corporation has become "a key postmodern social form."[4]

Kapor and Jobs are perhaps as well known for their drug experimentation and their interests in Eastern mysticism as for their influence in the computer industry. *Cyberia: Life in the Trenches of Cyberspace,* Douglas Rushkoff's book about the origins of the computer counterculture, quotes one of Apple's first engineers, Dan Kottke, discussing how he and Jobs "used to take psychedelics together" during Apple's early days, and discussed "transcendentalism and Buddhism and listened to Bob Dylan."[5] Kapor, meanwhile, joined forces with John Perry Barlow, a former lyricist with the Grateful Dead, to create the Electronic Frontier Foundation, which promotes civil liberties for computer hackers in cyberspace. The very name of Kapor's company—Lotus, named after the flower upon which the Hindu god Vishnu reclines as "preserver of the cosmos"—reflects the spiritual influences of Eastern religion in Kapor's life.[6]

In the church, the aging idealists of the sixties and seventies are rapidly becoming the elders of the traditional church. Although the "contemporary" format of boomer-oriented churches is anything but traditional to their generation, younger generations tend to find it dull, stodgy, and less than innovative. The baby boomers' role in the church has changed as well. No longer are they the idealistic world-changers of their youth. Today they are the church's authority figures, the keepers of the status quo. But as the first generation to be immersed in popular music, television, and movies, they have endued their churches with a good dose of "youth culture," even if it is not so youthful to the generations that follow them. Moreover, as the first generation to grow up surrounded by electronic media—namely, television—boomers also are comfortable with technology and have introduced technology into the church. Sophisticated sound systems, television monitors, and multimedia presentations are now fairly common accoutrements in boomer congregations.

Boomers also show an increasing interest in the Internet, especially as more businesses and families go online. But whereas later generations simply take the existence of the Net for granted, boomers must adapt to the technology. As Internet philosopher Sherry Turkle, herself a baby boomer, puts it, "Today's children are growing up in the computer culture; all the rest of us are at best its naturalized citizens."[7] Younger generations intuitively understand the workings of the Internet, but boomers often struggle with it. Little wonder, then, that some of the church's most vocal critics of the Net are members of the baby boom generation.

Generation X

Eirene belongs to that enigmatic demographic cohort known as Generation X. Perhaps even more analyzed than their boomer predecessors, Xers are generally portrayed as the photonegative of boomers. Indeed, such stereotypical characterizations oversimplify this generation. But there are certain assumptions about them as a whole that we should consider to understand better their ideas and ideals and how they contrast with those of N-Geners.

Xers are likely to challenge their elders on all fronts, questioning—even parodying—boomer values of idealism and materialism. They are a "survivor generation," writes youth minister Winkie Pratney. Sixteen million of their generation were aborted, and "Those who survived the war of the womb were forced to live through the breakdown of the nuclear family."[8] Now in their twenties and thirties, many Xers were the "latchkey kids" who grew up in single-parent households in the seventies and eighties. They're often seen as "alone," "abandoned," and "alienated."[9]

The disintegration of the family, which they witnessed in their formative years, has left them with "a self-confessed need for community and relationship," and many of them "idealize what it would be like to live in community."[10] That could be one underlying reason for the success of a favorite Xer TV show, *Friends,* which "is all about a group, a community, a team."[11] Unlike their idealistic boomer predecessors, Xers are pragmatists.[12] But they are alienated pragmatists who feel they live in the boomers' long shadow. In Rick and Kathy Hicks's words, Xers are generally "world-class skeptics, cynical about mankind and pessimistic about the future."[13]

In the early nineties, when the media began analyzing Xers in earnest, news magazines proclaimed Kurt Cobain, leader of the Seattle grunge band Nirvana, the pop culture icon for this generation. In typical Xer fashion, Cobain, who killed himself in 1994, was reluctant to take up the mantle. Yet Nirvana's dark anthems, particularly the song "Smells Like Teen Spirit," exuded the angst and despair that had come to define the generation. In yet another comparison of Xers to the baby boomers, Cobain was even called "the John Lennon of his generation."[14]

If Xers felt the world was filled with despair, they found comfort in technology. Reared on television, Gameboys, Walkmans, and personal computers, Xers are the first generation to come of age with the Internet. They often find solace in cyberspace. For them, the online world is ideal for discussing their thoughts on music, politics, social issues, and matters of faith. For many boomers, television was the medium that brought world-shattering events like the Tiananmen Square massacre and the fall of the Berlin

Wall into their homes in 1989. But for many Xer college students, the Net made them more than passive observers of these historic events. The Internet made them vicarious yet intimate participants in history.

"I sat in disbelief at my computer," writes Tom Beaudoin, a college student at the time of the Tiananmen Square demonstrations in Beijing, "as text from friends in China scrolled furiously before me, telling of tanks that rolled past their rooms and of students who were gunned down. I also communicated through e-mail with friends while the Berlin Wall was reduced to souvenir rubble. West German correspondents wrote me with fingers still tingling from taking a sledgehammer to Cold War concrete."[15]

The Net allowed Beaudoin and other college students to be part of the "global village" without the interference of a mediator. Thanks to electronic mail and chat rooms, people from half a world away were able to communicate in "real time" and without censorship. College students were able to bypass the institutional channels of information exchange. The Net became an unmediated medium. For many Xers, who exhibit a distrust of and skepticism toward institutions such as the news media, the government, schools, and the church, this is one of the most appealing aspects of the Internet. No authority figure stands between the two parties communicating.

"One of the things I think my generation stands for is a higher level of genuineness," says an Xer named Gary. "That's why the Internet is so popular: there's no facade, it's a WYSIWYG (what-you-see-is-what-you-get) environment."[16]

When it comes to the institution of the church, Xers find much lacking. "The church . . . is seen as being, at best, an outdated dinosaur of an institution and, at worst, a mean-spirited, close-minded hate group," write Todd Hahn and David Verhaagen. "For many it has become a thing to avoid, even oppose."[17] Beaudoin, whose book *Virtual Faith* examines the influence of pop culture on religion, echoes Hahn and Verhaagen's thoughts. While he was growing up, Beaudoin writes, the church "seemed hopelessly out of touch" to many in his generation. Church services were plagued with "hopelessly droll music, antediluvian technology, retrograde social teaching, and hostile or indifferent attitudes toward popular culture."[18]

Not all Xers have written off the church as a lost cause. But they often find little encouragement among entrenched church leaders who seem to resist change or who feel threatened by this younger generation's skeptical, questioning nature. Gen Xer Gary has tried to get involved in a local church, but he laments the reluctance of congregations "to try new things, or to experience their faith in new ways." He also feels shut off from the church leadership. "Some churches won't even acknowledge your existence until you have gray hair!" His notion of the ideal church is one that, in today's vernacular, "keeps it real" by fostering meaningful relationships, open discussion of spiritual issues, and "substantive and satisfying opportunities for involvement."[19]

Sadly, if any generation is lost to the modern American church today, it is probably Generation X. They continue to feel shut out of mainstream religion. Many of them turn to the Internet—and to New Age, pagan, and Eastern religions—for spiritual guidance. The church can perhaps reach many of them through cyberspace, if we can manage to keep it real.

The Net Generation

The unnamed teenager, steeped in the postmodern philosophy of our day and growing up in this digital age, represents the emerging Net Generation. Open and flexible, inquisitive, and comfortable with technology, she shrugs her shoulders and says cyberspace is just as good a place to worship God as any church. *I don't think it matters where you are or who you are with. If you are worshiping God, then you are worshiping God.*

Many in the church see the N-Geners as simply an extension of the skeptical, alienated Generation X. These church leaders are as confused about how to bring them into the fold—or, more important in their formative years, how to keep them in the fold as they mature—as they are about the generation that preceded them. But

N-Geners are *not* Xers, and the sooner the church realizes that, the better off the church will be in relating to both generations.

What sets this new generation apart from previous generations is the age into which its members have been born: the digital age. "Already these kids are learning, playing, communicating, working, and creating communities very differently than their parents," writes Don Tapscott in *Growing Up Digital.* "They are a force for social transformation."[20]

A Transformation in the Church?

Indeed, N-Gen is poised to transform society in ways even their boomer and Xer parents could not imagine. They also are growing up in a world that is markedly different than anything we've seen before. Theirs is a postmodern, multicultural, global, networked society, and the forces sweeping our cultural landscape today— forces that N-Geners accept matter-of-factly as "just the way things are"—pose dramatic challenges for the church.

Just how critical a time is this for the modern church? According to Christian sociologist George Barna, the church is now at a very crucial point in its history. Noting that our influence in society has been eroding for quite some time, Barna says that the church stands at "a crossroads" and must choose between two paths. The church must choose between defending the traditional structure, which impedes effective ministry, or embarking on a new path "that allows it to conform to its biblical mandate and still respond to the practical needs of its members."[21]

The trouble with many of today's churches, say Barna and other observers, is that they seem incapable of recognizing the extent to which the digital age influences young people. They also seem unable to see the need to venture into new realms—such as cyberspace— to reclaim Christianity's influence in culture and society.

To engage the Net Generation, the church must develop new approaches. As Barna further explains, "Their [the Net Generation's] heavy diet of mass media, combined with the uncritical embrace of computer technologies and the national shift in morals and values, has resulted in an entirely new filter through which Americans receive and interpret information. Whether we applaud or oppose that filter is not the issue at hand: The mere emergence of the new filter mandates a new style of sermon or lesson development and delivery."[22]

Which brings us back to cyberspace and that chat room discussion among members of three very different generations. One of the most interesting things about that gathering was not the topic of discussion but the fact that all three generations were converging in one place—albeit a virtual place—to discuss anything at all. Could such a discussion happen anywhere besides cyberspace? Perhaps. But how often do we find boomers, Xers, and teenagers coming together in our churches in common worship—let alone to engage in a meaningful discussion? All too often in America's churches, we segregate, or compartmentalize, our generations. The teens have youth group meetings, children are ushered in to Sunday school, the twentysomethings gather together for special "young adult" services, and the boomers are busy trying to orchestrate it all.

Could it be that cyberspace is one way to bring the generations together?

. . . .

eConnections: Online Resources for eMinistry

Bridging the Generation Gap

Take seven Web surfers, ranging in age from their teens to their sixties, give them a Web site through which they can share their thoughts, and you have the Generational Inquiry Group (GIG). These seven Netizens talk about their generations, and other generations, in writings about music, culture, government, technology, education, and other topics. Visit the GIG's Web site (www.millennials.com) for a glance at how these seven strive for intergenerational understanding.

Connecting Teens and Parents

Visit Walt Mueller's Center for Parent/Youth Understanding (www.cpyu.org) for ideas on how teens and parents can connect. The online excerpts from the CP/YU's quarterly newsletter, *youthculture@2000,* are also worth a read (www.cpyu.org/newslttr .html).

Another Multigen Resource

Explore "Reaching the Generations for Jesus" (home.pix.za/gc/ gc12/index.htm) to read some excellent articles, particularly about Xers and N-Geners. The site is the creation of Graeme Codrington, a computer consultant and youth minister in Johannesburg, South Africa.

Boomers, Unite

If all this talk about Xers and N-Geners is getting you boomers down, head on over to The Boomer Cafe (www.boomercafe.com) for some fellowship with others from your generation.

CHAPTER FOUR

Po-Mo Gumbo

*In those days there was no king in Israel: every man did
that which was right in his own eyes.*
—*Judges 21:25 KJV*

"THE GRAND INQUISITOR," a central chapter in Fyodor Dostoevsky's
classic novel *The Brothers Karamozov,* presents a beautiful allegory
contrasting the nature of God's kingdom, as revealed by the Jesus
of Scripture, with the human-centered religion that exists in His
name. In "The Grand Inquisitor," the agnostic Ivan Karamozov
tells his devout brother Alyosha of a poem he's written. The poem
describes Christ's arrival in Seville during the height of the Span-
ish Inquisition. The Grand Inquisitor, an old and bitter cardinal,
discovers Jesus and has Him thrown into prison. The two then
meet in Jesus' cell, where the old man explains why Jesus must be
executed the following day. By withstanding Satan's temptation in
the desert, the Grand Inquisitor says, Jesus forfeited three great
powers—*miracle, mystery,* and *authority*—and saddled humanity
with the intolerable burden of freedom.

To remedy Jesus' "error," the old cardinal explains, the church "cor-
rected Thy work" by founding it upon "miracle, mystery and authority." "And men rejoiced that they were again led like sheep, and that

the terrible gift that had brought them such suffering was, at last, lifted from their hearts." The church's "work" must continue unhindered, the Inquisitor says, and therefore Jesus must be executed.[1]

Although many readers of Dostoevsky's allegory see it as an indictment of the church for its failure to follow Christ's example of unconditional love, one eighteen-year-old college freshman from the Los Angeles area thinks otherwise. In an essay she wrote for an English class and later posted on her Web site, she boldly asserts, "Dostoevsky makes a strong case against Jesus in 'The Grand Inquisitor': Jesus did not love humanity sufficiently to care for the greater good of the race." Her essay goes on to present readers with a nontraditional take on the allegory—one in which the Grand Inquisitor becomes the hero and Jesus the villain.

And how does this student support her conclusion? Not by citing any literary criticism of Dostoevsky's writings, although tomes of such criticism are readily available at any college library or even over the Net. To describe the nature of God, does she turn to the Bible or any traditional writing? No. Instead, she borrows a line from Douglas Adams's popular novel, *The Hitchhiker's Guide to the Galaxy:* "'I refuse to prove I exist,' says God, 'for proof denies faith, and without faith I am nothing.'" She also sprinkles her essay with musings from shock-rock musicians like Marilyn Manson ("the weak ones are there to justify the strong," a line from the song "The Beautiful People") and concludes with a thought from anti-Christian philosopher Friedrich Nietzsche—that "the single thing more harmful than any vice ('sin') is 'active pity for all the failures and all the weak: Christianity.'"[2]

In this young woman's view, every "source" cited in her essay is credible. No doubt her professor was impressed with this student's talent for weaving the thoughts of a nineteenth-century nihilist with quips from science fiction novels and gothic music into an anti-Christian polemic of a significant portion of one of the world's great novels. The fact that she ignored any literary criticism of *The Brothers Karamazov* in her defense of the Grand Inquisitor apparently does not matter. In her world, all opinions are valid, all sources are credible, and every voice merits a hearing.

Welcome to the world of *postmodernism*—a world in which the concept of objective truth has been shoved aside, along with the Judeo-Christian idea of a single God, creator of the universe. It is, in the words of Christian author David W. Henderson, "a world with no purpose, no center, no source, no hope."[3] This is also the only world N-Geners have ever known. The Net Generation is not only the first truly *digital* generation but also the first *postmodern* generation as well.

Few terms are as ill-defined as *postmodern.* Yet, it is the term most commonly used to describe the prevailing mind-set in our culture today. Although Christian critics may prefer to refer to today's world as "post-Christian," that doesn't cover all aspects of contemporary society. For postmodernism not only rejects the traditional Christian ideas about truth but also abandons the notion that science, education, or other institutions can provide a path to "truth." In the postmodern world, it seems, the only measure of truth is the individual. In other words, if something *seems* true to an individual, then it must *be* true—never mind what science, reason, the government, the university, the media, the church, the family, or the Bible say about it. Like the young author of the essay on Dostoevsky, we are free to choose to ignore any "traditional" schools of thought and instead choose our own interpretations, our own references, our own perspectives, our own paths—in life as well as in literature.[4]

Postmodernism—"po-mo" for short—extends the consumerist ethic of personal choice into the moral arena. Deciding what is "right" and what is "wrong" is no longer connected to any moral code; it becomes a matter of convenience, preference, price, and personal taste. "Anything to do with reason," writes Jimmy Long in *Generating Hope,* "becomes suspect in postmodernism because truth is not allowed, only preferences. People now believe only what they feel or experience."[5]

This thinking also takes advantage of our multicultural society to promote a permissiveness, often disguised as tolerance, in which we are expected to "tolerate" all manner of lifestyle choices. And Jesus' command to "love your neighbor" no longer applies in a world in which the self is the center. To borrow a thought from poet Walt Whitman, postmodernism celebrates the self. Everything else—friends, family, institutions such as marriage and the church, and even God—is pushed aside.

Writer Os Guinness captures the essence of postmodern thinking in the following passage from his book *Fit Bodies, Fat Minds.*

> There is no truth, only truths. There are no principles, only preferences. There is no grand reason, only reasons. There is no privileged civilization (or culture, beliefs, norms, and styles), only a multiplicity of cultures, beliefs, periods, and styles. There is no universal justice, only interests and the competition of interest groups. There is no grand narrative of human progress, only countless stories of where people and their cultures are now. There is no simple reality or any grand objectivity of universal, detached knowledge, only a ceaseless representation of everything in terms of everything else.[6]

The Christian ska group, The Orange County Supertones, puts the following spin on postmodern thought in lyrics of the song "Grounded."

> Wisdom and truth
> have been vandalized,
> by the unevangelized.
> No truth in a world
> that is randomized.[7]

A Not-So-New Philosophy

Despite its name, the postmodern philosophy is nothing new. The modernist West—"a tower of Babel/built on anti-philosophy/ Nietzsche in the West/and Krishna in the East," according to the Supertones[8]—is thought by some to be actually "pre-Christian." One observer claims the society we live in is "a culture that still has yet to hear about who we are and what we believe."[9] The postmodern "antiphilosophy" actually goes back even farther than the years leading up to Jesus' birth. The author of the Old Testament book of Judges succinctly defined this worldview millennia ago: "In those days Israel wasn't ruled by a king, and everyone did what they thought was right" (Judg. 21:25 CEV).

Today, we face a situation similar to that of the ancient Israelites. In our world today, the King of Kings no longer rules. No more is He the center of our lives. The individual is now god. Right and wrong have vanished. We patch together our own beliefs from whatever is convenient. In the words of another Old Testament writer, "Judgment is turned away backward, and justice standeth afar off: for truth is fallen in the street, and equity cannot enter" (Isa. 59:14 KJV).

The church has good reason to be concerned about the postmodern worldview; it opposes many of the Christian faith's central doctrines. The denial of objective truth is a direct attack on both traditional Christianity and the claims of universal reason, which grew out of the Enlightenment of the seventeenth and eighteenth centuries. The exaltation of the individual runs counter to Christianity's emphasis on community. Moreover, postmodern thinking about identity—that the "self" is not unitary but composed of many "selves"—opposes Christianity's assertion that identity is more than merely a psychological issue. As Christian author and pastor David Fisher notes, our identity is made complete in Jesus Christ. "Our identity must be filled with Christian content—that is, rooted in God, formed by Christ, and empowered by the Holy Spirit."[10]

At the postmodern inn, there is no room for the idea that Jesus Christ is God's only Son, the only mediator between God and humanity. Yet postmodernism gladly welcomes all sorts of heresy—from atheism to gnosticism, paganism, and computer-assisted "techno-shamanism"—in the name of tolerance and respect for diversity. Religion—or, more often these days, "spirituality"—is not a bad thing, the postmodernists say, as long as one party does not impose its religious beliefs on others.

The popular musician Jewel seems to capture the essence of

postmodern spirituality in the following lines from her song "Who Will Save Your Soul?"

> So we pray to as many gods as there are flowers
> But we call religion our friend.[11]

Or perhaps, as Coleman Luck puts it in a critique of the popular postmodern television program *Touched by an Angel,*

> The "God" of the Dark Ages is history. From now on you must spell "god" with a small "g." . . . Whatever you do, don't personify "god" by naming him. Forget Krishna or Buddha or Yahweh or Jesus.[12]

Young people, steeped in this postmodern culture and heavily influenced by what the entertainment industry feeds them, pick and choose the ingredients of their own personal spirituality from a variety of belief systems. A kind of eclectic spirituality is in vogue these days, and it is a predictable outcome of the postmodern ethos. As one Christian magazine columnist notes, Hollywood's influence spills over to the youth culture: "Madonna has discovered cabala; Oprah is channeling the dead. Tom Cruise and John Travolta crusade for scientology. Actor Richard Gere embraces Buddhism, and many of our teens embrace reincarnation."[13] This approach to all things spiritual signals a shift toward "an experiential faith," a feel-good religion that "downplays doctrine and dogma," and "revels in direct experience of the divine."[14] It's a self-centered, "practical and personal" faith form, "more about stress reduction than salvation, more therapeutic than theological. It's about feeling good, not being good. It's as much about the body as the soul."[15]

"Many people seem to be looking for a postmodern faith offering a form of spirituality that makes little demand for serious change in their lives," writes Tom Sine. "That is why various New Age religions and Scientology are more popular today than the more demanding religions of the Moonies or the Hare Krishnas."[16]

Many young people today approach spirituality much as they

would a buffet. In *Reckless Hope: Understanding and Reaching Baby Busters,* Todd Hahn and David Verhaagen write of a young man who describes his beliefs to a local radio station thus: "I'm a born-again Christian. Yeah, I believe that Jesus was the Son of God. But I'm also a practicing Buddhist."[17] Similar interests in paganism and mysticism among young people are described by Tom Beaudoin in *Virtual Faith: The Irreverent Spiritual Quest of Generation X.* "As one GenX friend observed, 'My spirituality is drawn from Hinduism, Buddhism, Christian and Muslim mysticism, and Native American religions.' With these words, she summarized dozens of my religious conversations with Xers."[18]

Even churchgoing kids are drawn to this mix-and-match spirituality. Mike, a seventeen-year-old from upstate New York who frequently chats about religion with friends on the Internet, says he is "supposed to be a Roman Catholic, and a good one at that." He attends church regularly and is president of the youth group. But he questions the church's teachings on creation, heaven and hell, and other topics, and concludes, "Not only do I not believe that strongly in my own religion, but I can't even come up with a clear definition of 'My religion.'" His online friends "are also completely unsure about religion," he writes in an e-mail message. "Chicorina says 'catholic with buddhist tendancies' Jester says, 'everything, and yet nothing,' and Yajba is just confused. So there you go."

Beyond Black and White

The term *postmodern* was coined in the 1950s by English historian Arnold Toynbee, who "sensed the arrival of a new age or at least a new stage in modernity's decline."[19] But the postmodern worldview as we now know it has its roots in the nineteenth-century philosophies of Friedrich Nietzsche and others who began to dismantle the modernist worldview long before Toynbee attempted to write about it.

Modernism, which came to the forefront during the Renaissance and blossomed during the Enlightenment, emphasized science and reason over the God-centered, mystical worldviews that had developed throughout the church's early days. Although modernists rejected the faith-focused, biblically based perspective of the medieval church, they retained the church's universal, transcendental ideas of truth, beauty, freedom, justice, equality, and progress.[20] "The modern worldview was shaped by the Western assumptions of the inevitability of progress, the invincibility of science, the desirability of democracy, and the unquestioned rights of the individual," writes theologian Daniel J. Adams. "It was assumed that 'West is best' and that all other cultures of the world would eventually adopt Western values which would, with the passage of time, become universal."[21]

From its earliest days, modernism had an uneasy coexistence with Christianity. Some modernists wanted to strip the Christian faith of all mystery and reduce God to a series of mathematical formulas. Scientist-philosophers such as René Descartes and Isaac Newton, meanwhile, did not see any reason to bother with God at all. They "had no time for mystery" and were even hostile to it. Newton, for instance, equated mystical thought "with ignorance and superstition."[22] Descartes's famous declaration "I think, therefore I am" ushered in "a new premise for philosophical thought: man, rather than God, became the fixed point around which everything else revolved."[23] That philosophical idea gave birth to modernism and changed the Western world forever.

Postmodernism is not always so outwardly hostile toward the Christian faith. On the surface, it seems to embrace all things spiritual. It's an approach that Louis Dupré, a professor of philosophy at Yale University, calls a "new attitude of benign atheism." Contemporary society "shows a surprising openness to religion," Dupré writes, but "this interest rarely surpasses the purely horizontal, cultural level."[24] In other words, interest in spiritual matters is often merely "on the surface." Few people take this curiosity about religion below the surface in a quest for deeper meaning. That's one reason New Age religions have gained popularity in recent years. In New Age consciousness, writes Paul Lakeland, author of *Postmodernity: Christian Identity in a Fragmented Age*, "we find the trappings of religion without the heart—New Age religion is frequently intellectually

empty, bereft of tradition, at the mercy of sentimentality, incapable
of critique, blind to anything beyond the individual."[25] For most
westerners, Dupré concludes, "Christianity has become simply one
element of civilization among many others, and by no means the
most important. As a result, the unifying element of culture has
been lost and our vision of reality has become fragmented."[26]

A Spiritual Smorgasbord

Western civilization, built on the foundations of Judeo-Christian
heritage, now "appears to have said its definitive farewell to Christian culture," writes Dupré.[27] This is especially evident in cyberspace,
where, as one writer aptly put it, "the reigning beliefs of cyberculture are post-Christian, globalistic, and unitive."[28]

Many people see the computer and computer software as tools
to usher in a postmodern age. Larry Wall, for example, author of
the Perl programming language used to design forms, search engines, and other features on the Web, calls his creation "the first
postmodern computer language."[29] Postmodern sociologist Sherry
Turkle says computers—and, by extension, the Internet—"embody
postmodern theory and bring it down to earth." She calls the computer "an actor" engaged in "a struggle between modern and
postmodern understandings."[30]

But what exactly does Turkle mean? Go to any search engine on
the World Wide Web, and you'll quickly discover this "struggle"
for yourself.

Type in the word *angels,* click the button on your screen, and
watch what happens. A list of hundreds of sites materializes, seemingly in random order. One of the first links on your list might be
the "Angel Ring," which connects you to a host of cyber-cherub
sites. Few of the Angel Ring's Web pages, however, have much to
do with the traditional Judeo-Christian view of celestial beings.
Instead, you'll find special messages from these messengers on Web
sites such as "Prophecies of Aka, spiritual messengers of God,"
"Ask Your Angels," "Angels, Spirit Guides and the Fallen Ones,"
"Angel Encounters," and "Angelic Guidance—Free to Everyone."

Spirituality is hot in cyberspace, and the Internet offers online seekers a variety of choices. Many of the selections in this all-you-can-believe buffet are nontraditional. They are neopagan, pantheistic, New Age amalgams that borrow heavily from Eastern mysticism and the occult. All belief systems are on equal footing in cyberspace. As publishing and editing consultant Eric Stanford explains, "Cyberspace is accessible to all. It has no hierarchy. It won't distinguish between true and false, right and wrong. It has no beginning or end. It has an almost spooky intangibility to it. It's the perfect vehicle for the ideas underlying postmodernism."[31]

Perhaps the most famous example of how such religions use the Internet to spread their message is the story of the Heaven's Gate cult. In the spring of 1997, the cult's thirty-nine members committed mass suicide in their misguided attempt to reach the "level above human." Although the cult didn't originate in cyberspace, members used the Net to publicize their bizarre beliefs. The Heaven's Gate Web site described the cult's doctrine—a mixture of Christian eschatology and myriad New Age beliefs—in great detail. How many online seekers surfed into the Heaven's Gate site and discovered some new doctrine to try out? How many, moreover, have logged on to one of the many religious parody sites, such as the Church of the Bunny, only to click on that site's link to a "somewhat more serious" Webchurch, the Universal Life Church, proceeded to read the church's two open-ended tenets—"the absolute right of freedom of religion and to do that which is right"—and then downloaded the instant ordination that site offers?[32]

Writer Jeff Zaleski's prediction that the Internet "will break down the boundaries between religions" is right on target. The World Wide Web's hypertext design is particularly suited to postmodern rootlessness; everything is connected to everything else in no particular order. This nonhierarchical network approach favors loosely organized, flexible organizations and puts more rigid organizations at a disadvantage. "With a click of a mouse," Zaleski says, "I can leap from a Roman Catholic reading room to an Orthodox Jewish discussion group to an on-line meeting with a Zen master." As a result of this faith-surfing, "People will say, 'I believe in a lot of religions,'" instead of identifying with just one.[33] This approach, writes Tom Beaudoin, "leads to a 'relativizing' of religions and their truth claims for those in cyberspace. That is, someone surfing the Net can easily access any number of religions, which raises the question of their relative equality."[34]

This emerging cyberspirituality "doesn't have any anchor in a traditional religion," says media expert Quentin J. Schultze. "Whether or not this is going to lead people into the Christian faith is still open, depending on what Christians do with the medium."[35]

Online Missionaries

So, what *are* Christians doing with the medium? How should Christians approach this virtual world that rejects absolute truth?

Despite the dangers of postmodernism, the current culture does present some fresh opportunities for Christianity. During the age of Enlightenment, traditional Christian faith was seen as an enemy of reason. But with the emergence of postmodern thought, reason "has been taken down from its supreme position," and people might be more open to the Christian faith today than they have been in many years.[36] Moreover, while pessimism seems to characterize the postmodern worldview, "the postmodern generation's lack of contentment can lead it to seek new meaning in life."[37]

"There is a moral vacuum at postmodernity's core that cries out for filling," Leonard Sweet writes in his book *SoulTsunami*.[38] And despite postmodern culture's hostility toward Christianity, people are still open to Jesus Christ. "There is something about the person of Jesus that fascinates postmoderns—partly because they sense instinctively that he was one of them."[39]

The church needs to reclaim this radical, "pre-modern" Jesus and present Him to the postmodern world. What better place to start than on the Net?

The Internet is like a global mission field, ripe for the harvest. If we are to be missionaries to the Internet, however, we first must understand its culture. This means that we must immerse ourselves in cyberculture, understand its habits and customs, its language, and its worldview. Only then will we be ready to become Internet missionaries.

. . . .
eConnections: Online Resources for eMinistry

How Will You Stand if You Don't Understand?

Listen to the song "Grounded," by the Orange County Supertones, from their Web site (www.supertones.com). (The song is accessible from the site's virtual "jukebox." You can also read the lyrics on the Web site.) What does this song say about the postmodern worldview? What response do the Supertones advocate in this song?

Resources for the Postmodern Church

A great starting point for a journey into postmodern resources on the Internet is Canadian minister Jordon Cooper's Web site, "Resources for the Postmodern Church" (www.jordoncooper.sk.ca). Spend some time surfing around there.

A Po-Mo Primer

For a quick overview of postmodernism, from the quirky perspective of *Re:generation Quarterly,* read "Be a Postmodernist . . . Or Just Talk Like One!" It's available on the quarterly's Web site at www.regenerator.com/5.1/postmod.html.

Responding to Consumerism

Listen to the song "New Way to Be Human" by Switchfoot and follow along with the lyrics. (Both the lyrics and the song are online at www.switchfoot.com.) What does this song say about the consumerist ethic of postmodern society, and what, according to Switchfoot, should be the Christian response?

PART 2

Digital Life

CHAPTER FIVE

Religion, Politics, and Sausage-Making

Dear friends, you are foreigners and strangers.
—*1 Peter 2:11* CEV

ON SEPTEMBER 21, 1998, in the wake of special prosecutor Kenneth Starr's report on President Bill Clinton's sexual relationship with Monica Lewinsky, the writer of an online daily devotional posted the following commentary about the president's actions to several Internet discussion groups.

> If you are a Christian, you must forgive.
> Scripture is totally clear on this point. Many hypocrites consider themselves Christians, but they are not Christians, merely pretenders.
> Jesus says, "If you love me, keep my commandments." His commandment is that we must forgive. Period.

Bill McGinnis, whose online "Internet Daily Chapel" is sent electronically to a subscription list of hundreds and also appears on his Web site (www.patriot.net/users/bmcgin/chapel.html), fired off this Net sermonette to the Usenet discussion forums *alt.religion .christian, alt.bible, alt.politics.clinton, alt.president.clinton,* and *alt.impeach.clinton.* Subscribers to his daily e-mail received the same online admonition.

On the Usenet newsgroups, McGinnis's message met with all manner of responses, including the following.

> You cannot forgive someone who does not feel they have done wrong.

> To impeach or not to impeach has nothing to do with forgiveness.

> I forgive Mr. Clinton and wish him well. However, I think it's best if President Clinton resigns or is impeached.

> Forgiveness is the Way of Christ.

> When I see a thread calling for forgiveness for the supposed evils of Ken Starr, then I'll believe that this isn't just another ploy to deflect from Clinton's perjured testimony.

> Jesus teaches, "Render unto Caesar that which is Caesar's, and render unto God that which is God's." Impeachment is rendering unto Caesar, forgiveness is rendering unto God. . . . Maybe you believe that Schmucko's actions were divinely inspired. I wouldn't be surprised from reading some of the posts on these news groups.

Growing up, I was taught that there were three things polite people never discussed at the dinner table: religion, politics, and how sausage is made. With the online banquet of ideas known as the Internet, however, that rule does not apply in the case of at least two of those three subjects. Netizens freely discuss their views on religion and politics in online forums. They post their opinions on Web sites and freely chime in on bulletin board discussions related to almost any topic imaginable. Freedom of speech is one of the online world's most cherished values, and almost everyone on the Net, it seems, feels compelled to exercise this freedom.

McGinnis's hide is apparently thick enough to handle such critiques of his writings, for he continues to send his thoughts out to the Internet universe. If one is to participate in the rough-and-tumble community of Usenet newsgroups, one must be willing to put up with such harsh criticism online. On the Internet, the conventions of polite conversation do not exist.

Life in the Virtual Marketplace

In viewing cyberspace as a new kind of mission field—one with a culture all of its own—it's important to understand this online society. This virtual marketplace of ideas is truly postmodern in at least one sense: anyone's opinion is as valid as anyone else's. The Christian faith competes with a plethora of other voices in this online environment, and the anonymous nature of online discussions makes the Net an ideal milieu for free expression.

The online world is shaped by the consumerist, multicultural, pagan worldviews that define today's postmodern society. The value systems of many Netizens differ radically from the virtues espoused by the church. It's important, then, for Christians to understand this value system. To be salt and light in this new medium, Christians must approach the Internet with a missionary's perspective, learning as much as possible about this population before setting out to minister.

It's important to ask ourselves a few questions about cyberculture, including the following.

Who's Online?

Nobody really knows just how many people are connected to the Net. It's apparently impossible to take an accurate census of the online world. One of the more conservative studies predicts that the United States alone will have 135 million users hooked up to the Internet by 2001.[1] That total would nearly double the number of Americans who were estimated to be on the Net in 1998.[2] Another study expects 56 percent of North American households to be online by 2003.[3] Regardless of how many are online, one thing is certain: as the Internet continues to grow in popularity, its population will become more diverse.

Already, this diversification is changing the nature of cyberspace. The Net was once the domain of upper-income, predominantly male computer geeks and hackers, and their interests and attitudes helped to shape virtual culture. Today, the Net population is more balanced by gender, age group, income levels, and ethnicity. Women over fifty are the fastest-growing group of Americans logging on. Minority groups are also making large gains in Internet use.[4] This diversification means that the Net will become more and more a reflection of our "real" world—reflecting the diverse interests, tastes, and preferences of its inhabitants.

More and more of these inhabitants see Internet access as a necessity—a point driven home by a 1998 study by America Online and Roper Starch. According to that study, two-thirds of online users surveyed would prefer an Internet connection over a telephone or television if they were stranded on a desert island. Nearly half of those polled found the Internet a necessity, and three-fourths believe that their lives are better because of the Internet.[5]

The most cybersavvy Netizens are the young, as pointed out in Forrester Research, Inc.'s 1999 study, "The Net-Powered Generation." Forrester's survey of North Americans between the ages of sixteen and twenty-two found that they

- stay online longer than adults (an average of nine hours per week, 38 percent more than the average adult);
- connect from more places than adults (3.4 locations, versus 1.4 for their elders);
- do more activities online (such as downloading and listening to music, reading Webzines, and making phone calls over the Net) than adults; and

- are much more interested in high-speed connections than older Net users.[6]

How these N-Geners use the Net is creating new rules for the Web, the Forrester report points out. "Young consumers' online behavior puts them at the forefront of Internet adoption. But they are more than just advanced adopters—they have internalized the Internet and use it almost instinctively. As a result, this generation will embrace Net rules—far-reaching beliefs about the rights of the average consumer—that will reshape our economy."[7]

What's Their Language?

A missionary who travels to a foreign land with no understanding of the people's language is at a great disadvantage. The same is true in cyberspace. English is the dominant language on the Net, just as secular Western influence dominates Internet culture, but it is not always the spoken English with which most of us are accustomed. The keyboard language of the Net is informal, a kind of truncated, postmodern pidgin English. Forget all the rules of capitalization; names, titles, and other proper nouns are just as likely to be written with lowercase letters as with capitals. Also, cyberspeak is fraught with abbreviations. A typical chat room conversation might start out with "how r u" and end with "cul8r" (Netspeak for "see you later"), "brb" (be right back), "bbl" (be back later) or even "ttfn" (ta ta for now).

If you tell (type) a joke or (more likely for a *newbie* to the Net) do or say something stupid, expect to see chat denizens "lol" (laugh out loud) or "rofl" (roll on the floor laughing) at you. To avoid being lol'd at, newcomers to the online world should spend some time *lurking* (reading chat room and newsgroup messages before participating) and learning the slang. *Flaming,* for instance, is the term for sending heated, often sarcastic online messages. An exchange of those messages can escalate into a *flame war.* Then there are the *emoticons:* those sideways smiley faces—they look like this :-)—and other text-based symbols that Netizens use to convey emotion. The smiley indicates happiness and humor. Frequently, a winking smiley symbolizes sarcasm ;-). Regular users of the Internet also detest messages sent in all-capital letters, which is the digital equivalent of shouting.

Freedom of Expression

In addition to learning how to communicate on the Net, it's important to understand the nature of online communication. A lot of freewheeling discourse occurs in chat rooms and newsgroups. It might be advisable to stay in Christian-friendly venues for a while before venturing into the Net's more hostile, secular realm. But even Christian-oriented sites are not immune to argumentative flamers or raw language. Any discussion of religion, politics, professional sports, or other controversial issues is likely to raise the passions of participants—sometimes to the point of flame wars. Netizens are seldom timid about expressing their views. On the Internet, they somehow feel liberated from the conventions of polite conversation. This freedom of expression works for Christians, too, but we should not allow our freedom to become a license to conduct ourselves in the ungodly manner of many people in cyberspace. While we should feel free to express ourselves on any topic, for Christians, Proverbs 15:1—"a soft answer turneth away wrath" (KJV)—is a good rule to follow when conversing on the Net. If we can learn to disagree without being disagreeable, we will do well in cyberspace.[8] In all of our online dealings, we should heed Jesus' words to be as "wise as serpents, and harmless as doves" (Matt. 10:16 KJV).

What Is Their Identity?

One reason many people on the Net feel free to express their opinions is the anonymity of it all. In cyberspace, you are one of the faceless millions, a disembodied presence, simply text on a computer screen. This is the extreme view of how the Internet depersonalizes communication on the one hand and frees people on the other hand to be more expressive than they would be in person. The cloak of anonymity allows people to behave in ways that would be unacceptable in other settings. People also feel freer to explore taboo subjects. No doubt you've read about adult pedophiles logging on to chat rooms for children to lure kids into unsavory situations. Such scenarios are unlikely to happen in Christian forums, which are usually monitored and where rules of conduct are more stringent than in other parts of the online world. But even Christians are not immune to cybercharlatans who might use the Net to promote false ministries or argumentative types who want to discredit Christianity in various forums.

For young people who are uncertain about their spirituality, the Net's anonymity provides a nonthreatening interface for exploring the faith. Moreover, Christians who don't feel comfortable talking about their beliefs can be more assertive about sharing their faith in cyberspace. In many ways, witnessing online is easier than witnessing in "real life" (or RL, as it is called in Netspeak). The drawback is that no one can tell, based on a passing chat or e-mail exchange, whether a Christian really walks the talk. Therefore, it is important for Christians to present the faith honestly with online acquaintances, especially with those on the Net who are skeptical of Christianity.

Where Are They Now?

Another issue associated with the Internet is the ephemeral nature of the people, organizations, and services that sprout on it. If our life is like a vapor of smoke, as James 4:14 says, then life on the Net is hardly a flicker or a spark. Although it might be fairly easy to establish relationships on the Internet, maintaining them can be more difficult.

Nowhere is this ephemeral nature more evident than in chat rooms. Net "ministries" crop up overnight on chat channels. "Once the initial Internet fear has worn off," says Jenni Baier, webmaster for the Christian Internet Relay Chat Association (www.circanet.org), "people come to the Net with grand ideas of how it can be used for God, what kinds of huge ministries can spring up, how millions and millions will come to Christ—all wonderful ideas!" But these zealots don't take the time to find out what ministries already exist, and how they could work together with existing programs. "Instead," Baier says, "they work *against* them, trying to build up a ministry for themselves, in their name, with them calling the shots. Often the leaders of these 'ministries' are young (teenage) Christians or others who are not in a local church setting and are not accountable to any authority. Ministries come and go on the Net almost by the week—especially on IRC. Some channels will spring up, gain members by taking folks from other channels, flourish for a few weeks, then disappear as a new channel with new leaders springs up, taking members from *that* channel."[9]

What's New?

The rapid pace of change on the Internet tends to be overwhelming. New software, new Web sites, new chat rooms, and new forums seem to spring up overnight. It's difficult, at times, to resist the temptation to try to keep up with all of these changes.

Cyberspace: Peril or Promise?

Now that you understand a bit more about the nature of Internet culture, it's time to explore some of the issues confronting the church as we venture into this strange online world. The next chapter will examine some of the challenges of cyberspace and how we Christians should respond to them.

· ·
eConnections: Online Resources for eMinistry

Brush Up on Netspeak

Need a Netspeak refresher course? Then click over to Netlingo.com (www.netlingo.com) for the latest on Internet shorthand, acronyms, ASCII art, and smileys.

A Virtual Miss Manners

The Internet has its own peculiar code for acceptable behavior, known as "Netiquette." The sooner you learn some Netiquette, the sooner you'll connect with other Netizens. For starters, visit "The Net: User Guidelines and Netiquette" (www.fau.edu/netiquette/net/), developed by Arlene Rinaldi (who insists she is *not* the Miss Manners of the Internet) and Florida Atlantic University.

What Are They Searching For?

For a clue as to what's hot on the Internet, visit The Lycos 50 (50.lycos.com). Each week, Lycos compiles the fifty most sought-after topics in the Lycos search engine. Glancing at the top ten can give you insight into the hot topics of cyberculture (for the week, at least).

Getting the Big Picture

Stay ahead on Net culture with a Web site called "The Big Picture Stats Toolbox" (cyberatlas.internet.com/big_picture/stats_toolbox/article/). This site is a great one-stop source for all the latest in Internet trends and demographic information.

CHAPTER SIX

Cyberspace: Land of Peril, Land of Promise

If the LORD *delight in us, then he will bring us into this land.*

—*Numbers 14:8* KJV

To the casual observer, the Southern Baptist church in Georgia was thriving. But in the homes of some of its most stable families, a seductive new technology was taking its toll.

A church deacon entered the pastor's study one day with devastating news: his wife of nineteen years was leaving him and their two children for a man she'd met in a chat room. The virtual venue that led to this marital breakup was not one of those "cybersex" chat channels that pollute cyberspace. This particular Internet site was a Christian chat room.

The deacon was not the only church member to see his family break up with the help of the Net. Another deacon's eighteen-year marriage ended after his wife met a European man in a chat room. She left her husband and children to marry the man she'd met online. Then, a Sunday school teacher in that same congregation had to be removed from his teaching duties after developing an interest in online pornography. All of these problems led the church's pastor to conclude that the Internet is "destroying the fabric of what we stand for."[1]

Similar stories abound in today's news reports, as do accounts of a growing "Internet addiction" that draws people away from their families and communities. (Researchers conducted an online survey of more than 17,000 Internet users in 1999 and concluded that 6 percent of the Internet population—about 11 million Netizens—are "addicted" to the Net.)[2] Accounts also prevail of sexual predators lurking in chat rooms waiting to abduct unsuspecting children. Such reports are fairly common in today's newspapers, as the following examples indicate.

- In Texas, a married couple was arrested for luring, by using a chat room, a sixteen-year-old Michigan girl to Houston for a sexual encounter.[3]
- One man's Internet habit led him to spend more than a hundred hours online each week, ignoring his family and friends and stopping only to sleep.[4]
- In Denver, a man pleaded guilty to sexual assault for having sex with a fourteen-year-old girl whom he had met in a chat room.[5]
- A college student was so hooked on cyberspace that he stopped attending classes and flunked out. When he disappeared for an entire week, campus police discovered him in a university computer lab, where he'd spent seven days straight online.[6]
- In New Jersey, a man was sentenced to sixty-one years in prison for sexually abusing a fourteen-year-old girl whom he had met—you guessed it—on the Internet.[7]

The Internet does present a perilous new environment for our families, our spiritual lives, and our culture, and many well-meaning Christian leaders have been quick to point out the evils of this new technology. In his book *Virtual Gods,* author Tal Brooke, using near-apocalyptic tones, describes the Net as "a new theater of operations for what has been an ageless war over the human soul."[8]

He portrays it as the forerunner of "a very powerful beast" that "will be standing in the town square of history probably at the start of the next millennium."[9] Brooks Alexander, the founder of the Spiritual Counterfeits Project, sees cyberspace as a haven for New Age cults. He notes that "the computer revolution will greatly increase the number and power of available ways to flee from the presence of God—with particular emphasis on the more radical ways, such as techno-magic and digital spiritism."[10] From the foreboding tone of such writings, you'd think that nothing good could ever come from the Internet. But this "very powerful beast" *can* be used for God's purposes. Consider the following examples.

- A young woman devoted to the practice of witchcraft posted a message on a Christian bulletin board. She received a flurry of responses and began exchanging e-mail with a young man who explained the Christian faith to her. Within a few months, she became a Christian.[11]
- A teenage girl entered a chat room called *#chapel* one night and typed, "Can anyone help me?" Bill Tober, a retired Navy chaplain who runs the chat room, responded. The girl's father had just died of a heart attack. Tober and others in his online ministry got in touch with a minister in her city. The minister arrived at the girl's door within minutes to offer support and counsel. He handled all funeral arrangements for the family, and both the girl and her mother were baptized soon thereafter.[12]
- A volunteer organization decided to install computers in the homes of Alzheimer's victims to connect "spouses who feel isolated, overwhelmed, and hopeless." A true virtual community resulted, and the effort won the first community service award from the National Information Infrastructure Awards.[13]
- A man searching the Internet for homosexual pornography one night discovered a Web site called "We Love Homosexuals." He clicked on the site, which led him to a series of Scripture passages that pointed the way to salvation and an electronic

mail address to contact for help. He responded with an e-mail message, which went to a member of the Internet ministry of Word of Life Church in Wichita, Kansas. After receiving three weeks of online ministry through e-mail and chat, the man contacted a local minister and gave his life to Christ.[14]

Sex, Lies, and Cyberspace

As with any other medium, the Internet can be used for either good or evil. The popular media, however, seem to portray Internet occurrences as mostly evil. Increasingly, we read or hear about cyberporn, the spread of hate groups online, the dangers of computer hackers breaking into government databanks, and government and businesses monitoring Net users in big-brother style. Because the Net is unlike any other previous medium, it poses some new challenges. It is interactive, empowering users to connect with virtually anyone else online at any time and anywhere in the connected world. It is easily accessible, simple to navigate, and, at this point in its brief history, largely unregulated. All manner of information, both good and bad, is at our fingertips. But is cyberspace somehow more dangerous than print, radio, or television? Or is it just *different*, requiring us to take a new approach to the challenges it presents?

Cyberspace certainly has made pornography more accessible to minors. People meet online to engage in "cybersex." Net addiction is also a worry, as are the symptoms of social withdrawal that it might engender. In addition to these concerns, the Net poses other potential dangers, including the following.

Hate Groups Have Found a Home Online

Well-known racist organizations such as the Ku Klux Klan (KKK) use the Net to spread their propaganda and lure new members. Although most Americans are aware of the racist agenda of the KKK, the purposes of other online hate groups are not so obvious. Many people might not realize that online groups such as the Christian Identity Movement are racist; the use of the word *Christian* in that hate group's name can mislead unsuspecting surfers. Some sites even affiliate themselves with Christian causes. For example, well-meaning Christians interested in such social issues as abortion might stumble across a Web site such as "The Nuremberg Files," which has been alleged to promote violence against the abortionists that are listed. Any time one of the doctors on the list is slain, the Web site shows a line drawn through his name. Moreover, as we saw in the wake of the April 1999 school shootings in Littleton, Colorado, organized groups aren't the only ones using the Net to spread hate in cyberspace. Individuals drawn to racist, sexist, or anti-Semitic beliefs can easily promote their views over the Internet.

Dishonesty Is the Norm in Cyberspace

We've all heard about adults posing as children in chat rooms to lure kids into face-to-face encounters. But the nature of dishonesty in cyberspace is not confined to sexual predators. People online routinely lie about age, gender, occupation, and more intimate aspects of their lives. On the Net, it's easy for teens to pose as adults, for adults to pose as teens, for men to pose as women, and for couch potatoes to pose as star athletes. Recent studies indicate that half of all online users have given out false information on surveys. Such studies (if they are to be believed) reveal that "online identity and communication permit—and even promote—a certain shiftiness."[15]

The Net Hurts the Family and "Real" Community

Linked to anxiety about online addiction are concerns that the Internet is contributing to the breakdown of community and family life. Some Net critics contend that the online world pulls us away from our flesh-and-blood relationships. "The Internet is creating a class of people who spend more hours at the office, work still more hours from home, and are so solitary they can hardly be bothered to call Mom on her birthday," began a *Washington Post* report on Net addiction.[16] Such alarmist writing is common in not only the traditional press but also recent books. "While anonymous intimacy grows on the Internet," writes Tal Brooke in *Virtual Gods*, "friends and intimates in the *real* world are often put on hold as a new sort of addiction grows among those who have tasted the Internet."[17]

Computer Games Are Becoming Increasingly Violent

A few years ago, parents worried about violence on television. Now, the big business of computer games exposes kids to even more violent scenarios. A game called "Kingpin: Life of Crime" is billed as a "multiplayer gang bang death match for up to 16 thugs!" The ad copy promises gamers that they will "actually see the damage done, including exit wounds."[18] As Net technology matures, violent multiplayer games such as Kingpin will be accessible over the Web, allowing gamers half a world away to waste each other in real time.

The Net Bombards Our Souls

Isn't it enough that we come home from work or school to find our mailboxes stuffed with junk mail? Now, we log on to our PCs and find that mass marketers—or "spammers," as they're known in cyberspeak—have crammed our e-mail boxes with unsolicited messages. We receive electronic come-ons for everything from erotic Web sites to get-rich-quick schemes and "free" cruises. Even without Internet spam, the constant flood of information from online sources overwhelms even the most info-savvy of us. The Net contributes to the "noxious muck and druck of the information age," writes David Shenk in his book *Data Smog*. This overflow of data "gets in the way; it crowds out quiet moments, and obstructs much-needed contemplation."[19] And quietude is something that Christians—and everyone else—need desperately today.

The Net Fosters a "Digital Divide"

Some people fear that the rush toward computerization is creating a society of online haves and have-nots. The "haves" are mostly white and middle- to upper-income families in urban and suburban areas in North America and western Europe, where access to computer networks is plentiful. The "have-nots" are mostly nonwhite, low-income families who can't afford computers or Internet access, or people who live in remote areas where Net access isn't readily available. The digital divide, critics say, will favor those who have computers, leaving those without Internet access in the cold, dark, digitalless world. "America's digital divide is fast becoming a racial ravine," warned one U.S. Department of Commerce official upon the release of an in-depth study of the problem.[20]

The "Techno-utopians" Will Rule—and Ruin—Civilization

The titans of the information age have the most to benefit from promoting the idea that computers and connectivity will solve many of society's ills. Chief among them is Microsoft chairman Bill Gates, who waxes techno-messianic when he speaks of the Internet bringing "undreamed-of artistic and scientific opportunities to a new generation of geniuses."[21] The techno-utopians promote a wide-eyed optimism that ignores many of the real concerns that people have about cyberspace. After all, techno-utopians have a spotty track record when it comes to their predictions. For example, in 1940, the founder of the National Broadcasting Company proclaimed that television was a technology that was "destined to provide greater knowledge to larger numbers of people" and "a broader understanding of the needs and aspirations of our fellow human beings."[22] "The great lesson" from such pronouncements, David Shenk writes, is "beware of men bearing magical machines and a list of hopeful prophecies attached."[23]

Spying Out the New Promised Land

Although many of these concerns pose significant threats to the stability of our marriages, our families, and our society, they are no cause for undue fear. When it comes to cyberspace, Christians should not adopt a bunker mentality, hoping to hold out faithful against the rampant dangers of the online world. Instead, we should make every effort to use the Internet for good, not for evil. But we also must be as "wise as serpents, and harmless as doves" (Matt. 10:16 KJV) in our use of the Net.

Think of cyberspace as a kind of new promised land, and the church as akin to the children of Israel, who have been wandering in the wilderness. Just as Moses sent out twelve men from the twelve tribes of Israel to "spy out the land" of Canaan (Num. 13:17 KJV), so has God called several "spies" from the church to explore this new online world. Those of us who are called to scout cyberspace have a similar mission: to report back to the church about the place and to determine whether we should enter it.

In the Old Testament account, ten of the twelve spies returned with a negative report. Although they saw with their own eyes the potential of Canaan—this land "rich with milk and honey" (Num. 13:27 CEV)—the ten spies chose to focus on their fear of the uncertain. They didn't focus on the abundance of the land; they chose to focus on the inhabitants, whose culture and appearance differed significantly from their own. These men, who were accustomed to a nomadic lifestyle, observed that "the people who live there are strong, and their cities are large and walled" (v. 28 CEV). The inhabitants were "like giants" and were "so big that we felt as small as grasshoppers" (vv. 32–33 CEV).

But the other two spies, Caleb and Joshua, had another perspective. Tearing their clothes in sorrow, they told Moses and the people,

We saw the land ourselves, and it's very good. If we obey the Lord, he will surely give us that land rich with milk and honey. So don't rebel. We have no reason to be afraid

of the people who live there. The Lord is on our side, and
they won't stand a chance against us!

—Numbers 14:7–9 CEV

Today, we are hearing from both sets of spies who have entered
the world of the Internet. Some of them, like the ten Israelite spies,
speak of only the dangers. Some of them, the Calebs and Joshuas
of our day, urge us to enter into cyberspace. Which report shall we
believe?

We should heed the Calebs and Joshuas. The Internet is part of
God's unfolding creation. We are able to enter the land and be His
witnesses there.

Wise as Serpents, Harmless as Doves

As we enter this new promised land, however, we must use wisdom. Parents must be involved in helping their N-Gen children
learn to use the Net for good and not for evil. The key is an old-
fashioned virtue called communication. Parents, *talk* to your children about the concerns you have about the Net.

Online pornography is often the first concern a parent has about
the Internet. When it comes to the subject of porn, even the
staunchest defenders of free speech are likely to agree with Donna
Rice Hughes's assessment: "Defending minor children from harmful pornography goes beyond questions regarding censorship to
how society should behave responsibly in protecting children from
material that victimizes them."[24] Although the Children's Online
Protection Act, passed by Congress in 1998, goes a long way toward protecting minors from viewing harmful pornographic materials online, it does not fully shelter minors from virtual smut.
Kids can still access porn via newsgroups, and unmoderated chat
channels can be dangerous ground for young people who are exploring their sexuality. Clearly, parents must take an active role in
ensuring that their children are not only aware of the dangers but
also protected from those dangers.

What can parents do to ensure that their children are protected?

Installing filtering software on the family computer or subscribing to a Christian Internet service that filters the Web for its members is a good first step. Such filtering software will keep your kids from accessing inappropriate material. (Several filtering products and services are mentioned in the appendix of this book.) But parental guidance should not end there. A "Net-sitter" cannot be expected to solve every problem associated with online access. As Focus on the Family points out on its Web site (www.family.org), it is important for parents to be involved in their child's Internet experience. Walt Mueller, president of the Center for Parent/Youth Understanding, encourages the same approach. "With kids growing up computer-smart, it's important that parents take the time to investigate the new world of computers and the Internet," Mueller writes in *Understanding Today's Youth Culture*. He advises parents to "take the time to familiarize yourself with this new technology that is here to stay."[25]

Media critic Jon Katz suggests that parents enter into a "social contract" with their children to help promote responsible use of the Internet and other media.[26] Other organizations, such as Focus on the Family and America Links Up, offer more specific approaches to help parents and their children enjoy the Internet together. They include the following ideas.

- Keep the computer in an area where everyone can see how it is being used.
- Spend time with your children on the Internet and teach them to be discerning.
- Show them what to do if they accidentally stumble onto a dangerous Web site or chat room.
- Help them set up Web page "bookmarks" to help them find appropriate sites. (Several suggested bookmarks for kids and teens are listed in the appendix.)
- Set time limits on their Internet usage.
- Keep communication lines open with your kids. Ensure that your child feels comfortable talking to you if he or she stumbles into harmful online situations.[27]

By getting involved in our children's use of the Internet, by setting clear boundaries and guidelines for them, and by monitoring the amount of time that our kids spend on the Net, we can go a long way toward ensuring that our Net Generation's online experiences are positive. By doing so, we will be playing an important role in the process of "digital discipleship"—even if we ourselves rarely go online.

. . . .

eConnections: Online Resources for *e*Ministry

Taking on Internet Porn

The eXXit Web site (www.exxit.org) is an online ministry of Northwest Community Church of San Antonio, Texas, to help those struggling with online pornography. The site's three-minute Bible studies, updated daily, are designed to steer surfers away from sexual temptation. Visit the eXXit site and recommend it as a resource to someone struggling with online pornography.

Get Web Wise

Visit the Web Wise Kids site (www.webwisekids.com) for more ideas on how to help the N-Geners in your home safely navigate the Net. Go over "Rascal's 7 Smart Rules for Internet Safety" (www.webwisekids.com/rascals.html) with your kids. Parents, be sure to read "My Advice to Parents" (www.webwisekids.com/advice.html).

Closing the Technology Gap

For the latest on government initiatives to help close the technology gap, surf over to Closing the Digital Divide (www.digitaldivide.gov).

How You Can Help Bridge the Digital Divide

To do your part to help bridge the digital divide, why not donate your old computer to a school, church, missionary, or library? Or go to the "Donate Your PC" page of the Web site called Heaven (www.hubheaven.org/y2c/donate.html). This non-profit agency can connect you with groups in need of new or used computers.

Technology: Good, Bad, or Ugly?

When it comes to technology, do you tend to side with the techno-utopians, who see only the good that technology brings society, or with the techno-luddites, who see technology as ultimately threatening our world? For the perspective of one of the world's leading experts on technology, read media critic Neil Postman's speech, "Informing Ourselves to Death," available online from the Electronic Frontier Foundation (www.eff.org/pub/Net_culture/Criticisms/informing_ourselves_to_death.paper). Do you agree with Postman's assessment that "technological change is always a Faustian bargain," and that "[t]echnology giveth and technology taketh away, and not always in equal measure"?

PART 3

Digital Discipleship

CHAPTER SEVEN

Bibles, Bots, and Body Art

*I have become all things to all men, that I might by all
means save some.*

—*1 Corinthians 9:22* NKJV

IT'S A SLOW NIGHT ON *#Teens4Christ*, an Internet Relay Chat (IRC)
channel on the Undernet. Khan_Guru decides to try to liven things
up a bit. He tells his chat pals that he wants the image of Odie, the
puppy from the "Garfield" comic strip, engraved on his shoulder
blade.

But no one is going for Khan_Guru's flame bait tonight. LizLiz
responds by describing a similar desire for a permanent marking.
"I want a tattoo of a pic I've drawn," she says (types). "I would
want one as a permanent mark of my faith—kind of like the op-
posite of the mark of the beast."

"Well that's not the ONLY tattoo I want," Khan_Guru adds.
"One of those cool Hebrew ones that everybody was gettin a
Tomfest would be pretty cool . . . =) I wanna just walk in and say
'Gimme the Henery Rollins' ;)"[1]

```
<Nuzzle> I'm gonna get either my tongue or my
eye brow pierced next week!!!!
```

```
<Khan_Guru> Go for the eyebrow!
<LizLiz> i would got for the tongue most
definately
<Khan_Guru> Nah . . . the tounge is overdone.
<Khan_Guru> Eyebrow. =)
<ToMmY> why not staple your tounge to the in-
side of your cheek?
<JeSuSgRrL> ewww
<Nuzzle> see . . . If I get my tongue I can hide it
<LizLiz> lol
<ToMmY> nuzzle: get a genital piercing if you
want to hide it
<Khan_Guru> Yeah but the eyebrow is so much
cooler . . . =)
<NY_Paul> ToMmY . . . grow up
<Nuzzle> haha
<Nuzzle> I don't have the guts to do that.²
```

Many older Christians logging on to such a cyber-conversation might find it distasteful at best, if not downright sacrilegious and further proof that cyberspace is no place to leave one's child unattended. But seasoned sojourners of cyberspace know that discussions of tattooing, body piercing, and other forms of body modification ("bod mod") are commonplace in Christian N-Gen chat rooms. Bod mod fascinates N-Geners, Christian and non-Christian alike.

The marketing world knows this. That's why the latest incarnation of Barbie comes complete with nose ring and a butterfly tattooed on her stomach.[3] Tom Beaudoin's description of Xers as "a generation willing to have experience, to be profoundly marked, even cut, when religious institutions have not given us those opportunities" also applies to N-Geners.[4] By now, experts' predictions that tattoos would be the hottest Christian fashion accessory since WWJD bracelets has probably come to pass.[5] And who will be getting those tattoos? The same demographic cohort that snatched up all the WWJD and FROG fashion accessories: the Net Generation.[6]

Tattoo talk is not confined to chat rooms. Every few months, a question such as the following, which was posted on the Usenet newsgroup *rec.music.christian*, spawns interesting discussion:

> Howdy Folks, I'm thinking of getting new tattoo on my left arm (the right arm has the drawing from Shel Silverstein's "Hug o' War" poem). I want to get something to celebrate my new faith (one whole year), but I really don't have a clue. We've . . . thought about everything from Veggie Tales (Larry of course) to Hebrew letters to the "fish." Any and all suggestions, thanks

First came a suggestion: "How about the fish with the date you accepted the Lord under it?" Then a counter-suggestion: "Don't get a fish, that's tired. I'm pretty stoked with my Hebrew letters on the underside of my left forearm." Then came the "me too" postings: "All of this talk about a new tattoo makes me want to go get one. When I got my first one, the guy told me they were 'addictive'. LOL. I have Felix The Cat on my left leg, with Eccl. 3:4 under it. . . . you'd have to see it." The debate about body modification, and whether Scripture allows or forbids it, quickly followed. As soon as a poster made reference to Leviticus 19:28—which says, "You shall not make any cuttings in your flesh for the dead, nor print any marks upon you: I am the LORD" (NKJV)—the amateur theologians of *rec.music.christian* started cranking out their opinions and casting virtual stones at one another with abandon.

Through these muddied digital debates on body piercing, the following two things emerged clearly:

1. Bod mod *matters* to the Net Generation, both Christian and non-Christian.
2. The online church offers N-Geners scant guidance on the topic.

Right Answers, Wrong Questions

Some of the most visible and most respected apologists in the evangelical community have nothing to say online to the Christian youth who is curious about body piercing. For example, Josh McDowell is one of evangelical Christianity's better known apologists to the youth culture. The author of apologetics classics such as *Evidence That Demands a Verdict* and *More Than a Carpenter,* also has built an impressive presence on the Web (www.josh.org). So what does this well-known apologist's Web site have to say about body modification? Nothing.

What about the Christian Answers site (www. christiananswers .net), which claims to provide "free, accurate, biblical answers on a wide variety of questions on the minds of both Christians and non-Christians"? Again, nothing.[7] Answers in Action (www.answers .org), R.C. Sproul's Ligonier Ministries (www.gospelcom.net/ ligonier), Ron Hutchcraft Ministries (www.gospelcom.net/rhm)— all Web sites that claim to address the issues critical to Net culture—are also silent on this topic.

A quick cruise through the major search engines—type in any combination of keywords such as *Christian, tattoo, piercing, body art,* or *body modification*—also yields little fruit. The top site on many such searches is a young man's homespun Web site titled "The Truth About Christian Tattoos."

What is wrong here?

The questions to their answers, for one thing. All of these ministry Web sites have excellent, biblical responses to a diversity of issues. The problem is that many of their online databases contain answers to questions that few people in the Net Generation are asking. In other words, they have good answers, but they are for the wrong questions. Consequently, the answers aren't very good at all.

Even the most progressive online ministries seem to be clueless about the nature of the Internet culture they hope to influence. Few Christian Web sites have anything to say about bod mod, cults, sex, movies and music, the supernatural, computers, cyberculture, science fiction, or UFOs. Although news media reports focus on "pornographers, hackers and virus-makers," notes Jon Katz, who writes for the popular Web site Slashdot (slashdot.org), cyberspace sojourners have other things on their minds, including spirituality. "Next to sex and e-trading," Katz writes, "nothing keeps a search engine humming longer than typing in 'spirituality,' or 'religion.'"[8]

Perhaps the leaders of most online ministries don't think that body modification or UFOs are relevant to Christians. Yet, they are subjects that captivate many people in the online community. By ignoring them, the church risks becoming even more irrelevant among such people than it is already. A church that does not address the issues that matter to Net culture is worse than irrelevant; it is a church that ignores Jesus' instruction to be "salt" and "light" in the world (see Matt. 5:13–16 KJV)—and that world must include the realm of cyberspace. To borrow a term from Blaise Pascal, a "God-shaped vacuum" exists in the Internet when Christianity is not present and active. We can be certain that something—mindless entertainment, cyberporn, or the allure of other religious groups—will rush in to fill that void. In the words of one religion expert, "If churches won't address the interests and obsessions of real people—especially the young—then the cults and the alternative religions will."[9]

Formulating a Christian Response

The apostle Paul's ministry was focused heavily on meeting people on their own turf and relating the message of the gospel to their lives. The Athens of Paul's day was tough territory for an itinerant preacher. It was a city "given over to idols," and Paul's "spirit was provoked within him" because of it (Acts 17:16 NKJV). Yet, did he turn his back on the idolaters? No. He *related* to them. He went into their marketplaces. He went to Mars Hill, where the elite of Athens hung out to discuss the latest fads and fashions. When he spoke to them, he quoted one of their own poets, then he related the divine wisdom revealed in their own culture to the truth of the gospel (see Acts 17:17–34 NKJV). (If Paul were around today, from which of our many spiritually informed poets would he quote to the netizens of cyberspace? Alanis Morrisette, Beck, Public Enemy, or Sarah McLachlan? Kid Rock? Puff Daddy? Or maybe even—*shudder*—Marilyn Manson?)

To be relevant in cyberspace, the church must learn the culture. If bod mod matters to the Net Generation, then it had better matter to the church.

React.com: Keeping It Relevant

The editors of a Webzine called react.com (www.react.com), a publication for teens, knows the importance of being relevant to their N-Gen readers. The site's November 15–21, 1999, issue links to a Q-and-A feature with comedian Molly Shannon of *Saturday Night Live* fame, news (and a chance to comment) about the Harry Potter books, a roundup of news of interest to teens, and more. The issue also features an interactive quiz to help teens figure out— virtually—which style of tattoo might best fit their personalities.

"Want all the fun of tattoos without all the pain and suffering?" posts the quiz's author, Chris Tauber. "Close your eyes, turn on your imaginative powers and take react.com's Tattoo IQ Quiz (not necessarily in that order). By gauging your personality type, we guarantee to predict the perfect tattoo for you so you can make the right choice." The site then poses ten fun multiple-choice questions, including the following.

- When you change your style, you do it because:
  ___ It's Tuesday.
  ___ Just like eating oatmeal, it's the right thing to do.
  ___ Mr. Binky, that little voice in your head, told you to.
  ___ You saw it on Moesha.

- Which nickname is closest to yours?
  ___ Scooter
  ___ Bruiser

___ Cher
___ Psycho

- You will love your boyfriend/girlfriend until:
  ___ death do you part.
  ___ lunch.
  ___ you can trade up.
  ___ the universe implodes around you.

- Humongous needles pointed at your skin make you:
  ___ scream like a banshee.
  ___ giggle like a school girl.
  ___ curse like a sailor.
  ___ faint like a wuss.[10]

React.com's interactive approach—the site is "built for doing, not reading"—seems to resonate with N-Geners. The site garners some 6 million page views a month. Such sites, though not Christian in nature, can augment ministry approaches on the Internet. And ministries hoping to connect with N-Geners can certainly learn from sites such as react.com.

Back to the Bible?

The Bible is still the church's best hope for making disciples in the realm of the digital. But it also is one of the church's greatest weaknesses. The Bible is still the best-selling book in history, but our postmodern society is no longer a society that values the written word. As Paul-Gordon Chandler, head of the International Bible Society, explains,

> We are called a "People of the Book," yet ours is no longer a reading culture. Biblical illiteracy grows, both within and outside the walls of the church. As the world searches for a story by which to live its life, the greatest story ever told is known by fewer and fewer.[11]

Our challenge is to present the message of "the Book" in fresh, creative, and engaging ways in a culture that is increasingly Bible illiterate. The Christian church online must be built on the same rock-solid foundation as the offline church: "on the foundation of the apostles and prophets, Jesus Christ Himself being the chief cornerstone" (Eph. 2:20 NKJV). Only upon this foundation, the revealed spiritual understanding of God's kingdom through the Scriptures, can we begin to build true community and true digital discipleship in cyberspace.

. . . .

eConnections: Online Resources for eMinistry

Tattoo You?

Read "Tattoo or Not Tattoo: That Is the Question" (www.webpulse .com/sanctuary/message/pastor_dave/tattoo_not_tattoo/ tattoo_not_tattoo.html). Do you agree with the author? Why or why not? (The author, Dave Hart, is pastor of Sanctuary San Diego [www.webpulse.com/sanctuary], a church that ministers to San Diego's Goths.)

Bod Mod: Another Perspective

"Is It Appropriate for Christians to Practise Body Modification?" is the title of an editorial published in *Body Modification Ezine* (www.BME.FreeQ.com/news/edit003.html). Contrast the opinions expressed in this editorial with Dave Hart's comments. Which author presents the better case for a biblical approach to this issue?

Hip Hop Meets Scripture

Listen to the audio clip from the song "Everything Is Everything," by Lauryn Hill, from her CD "The Miseducation of Lauryn Hill," and follow along with the lyrics. (The audio clip and lyrics are online at www.lauryn-hill.com/music.html.) What is this modern poet saying to her generation? Do you think her music is directing listeners toward spiritual matters?

Talk of the Net

Take a trip to Deja.com's Usenet Discussion Service (www.deja.com/usenet/) to see what Netizens are talking about these days. If you're in need of some topic ideas, revisit The Lycos 50 (50.lycos.com).

CHAPTER EIGHT

The Word on the Web

In the beginning was the Word.
—*John 1:1* KJV

IF THE BIBLE IS THE church's greatest resource for communicating the love of God in cyberspace, it also is the church's greatest hindrance to engaging the Net Generation. This fact is not because the Bible is no longer relevant to today's culture but because the church has saddled the Word of God with many negative connotations.

The Bible likens Scripture to a two-edged sword (Heb. 4:12 KJV). Nowhere is this analogy more true than on the Internet, where the Bible cuts both ways, able both to pierce the soul of those who truly seek the truth and to cut the church off from the prevailing culture of the Internet. The message of the gospel is as relevant to Net culture as it is to any traditional churchgoer. Yet, in cyberspace, where "timeless truths" are measured in nanoseconds, the eternal Word has little influence.

If the church truly believes that the Bible holds the power to change lives, then we must make it a priority to introduce the Net Generation to this wonderful book. At the same time, we must understand that our much-loved "Good Book" must be transformed. It must be released from the tyranny of the printed page to reach a wired, digitized, hyper-connected world.

Young people seek spiritual truth, even if they seek it in ways that the traditional church sees as unconventional. A generation of multitaskers, accustomed to processing a barrage of messages that come to them with the rapidity of an MTV music video, have become expert editors who quickly filter out those messages they find unappealing.[1] This image-oriented generation will not take easily to the traditional church's modernist, logical, linear approach.

Still, the Bible offers great hope for introducing Jesus to the young. Latin American theologian Rodolpho Carrasco, a member of Generation X, describes that hope and the challenge to the church when he writes that "the age-old wisdom of the Bible can affirm my generation in all its complexity, while pointing to a greater, eternal harmony. But will the church be able to communicate this to us?"[2]

The church *will* rise to this challenge if it heeds the words of Paul-Gordon Chandler of the International Bible Society. "We need to effectively re-open the Book," he says, "and have non-Christians meet a Bible they never knew existed, leading them to consider the case for the Christian faith."[3]

This task won't be easy for a church conditioned by hundreds of years of "word-based" Christianity. While our postmodern culture celebrates the "triumph of the image"[4] over the written word, the traditional church is mired in Enlightenment-era rationality, a world in which "the word was the primary unit of cultural currency." In today's culture, where the image is the primary unit of cultural currency, the word-based church finds itself with a huge deficit.[5] Granted, much online communication is textual, but it is a different kind of text-based communication than that to which the church is accustomed. In cyberspace, "Even our common text, hypertext, behaves more like a picture—or an icon—than like a printed word."[6]

To reach the Net Generation, we must release the power of Holy Scripture from the confines of the book and present it in new ways. "Our challenge," Chandler writes, "is to release the Scriptures, to set them free to achieve the purpose for which they were sent."[7]

The Internet offers the church a wide array of opportunities to share Christ in a culture that is obsessed with image. Therefore, we should use the Net's video and audio capabilities as much as possible. The Jesus Film Project of Campus Crusade for Christ International, for example, has translated the global success of its "Jesus" film to the Net by uploading the two-hour movie of Christ's life and making it available on the Net in fifty different languages. The Internet site, www.jesusfilm.org, also provides an audio drama that allows visitors to hear "the greatest story ever told." Another encouraging effort to translate the Word for modern sensibilities is the International Bible Society's "Discovering Ancient Wisdom" Web site (www.discovering-wisdom.com). There, online seekers can discover the Old Testament truths from Proverbs and Ecclesiastes in contemporary English and listen to the magical guitar sounds of Phil Keaggy as they read the short installments. (Each "page" of the two online wisdom books contains only a few verses, and the books' names have been changed—Ecclesiastes has become "Pondering the Meaning of Life," and Proverbs is "Practical Words of Insight and Understanding"—in an effort to remove barriers to the Bible.)

Traditional organized religion is not the best vehicle through which to spread God's Word to postmodern N-Geners. As theologian Leonard Sweet points out, "There is a huge spiritual hunger and at the same time a rejection of Christianity as the kind of spirituality that can slake the spiritual hunger."[8] In true postmodern fashion, many N-Geners are fusing beliefs from many different religions and philosophies into their own personalized faith systems. Drawing from Eastern mysticism, the pop spirituality of Hollywood ("may The Force be with you"), and the music of our times (everything from the "girl power" of the Spice Girls to the nihilism of Marilyn Manson), N-Geners "are turning their backs on traditional religious expressions and creating new spiritual traditions and do-it-yourself spiritualities."[9]

Now, Hear the Word of the Lord. . . .

Today's connoisseurs of mix-and-match spirituality need to hear the "old, old story" in a fresh way, one that does not force the gospel down their throats. The church, then, needs to present the good news in a new way. To do that, we actually must step back in time and rediscover the early, premodern church's oral tradition. Ironically, the high-tech, high-text medium of the Internet presents us with this opportunity like no other tool.

Before the Bible became a book to be read, it was a collection of writings shared orally—and received aurally—among communities of believers. As Paul-Gordon Chandler explains,

> Stories were told and retold to gatherings of people. Psalms were sung in corporate worship. The law was read publicly at important national events. Prophetic warnings were thundered in the gates of Jerusalem. The words of Jesus were memorized and passed on to others. Letters by apostles were read at gatherings of the earliest Christ-followers. The people of God heard the Word of God long before they began to read it.[10]

New Testament Scripture confirms the importance of the spoken Word. Paul explained to the early church in Rome that "faith comes by hearing, and hearing by the word of God" (Rom. 10:17 NKJV). Eugene H. Peterson, who updates the language of Scripture for contemporary eyes and ears in the Bible paraphrase *The Message,* presents Paul's words in this fashion: "Before you trust, you have to listen. But unless Christ's Word is preached, there's nothing to listen to" (v. 17).

If cyberspace communication is still predominantly image- and text-based, how can the Word of God be "preached" over the Net? How can N-Geners "listen"?

Although it's true that life on the screen consists primarily of text, sometimes accompanied by still photographs and graphics, the "language" of the Net is not the language of the written word. This language—call it "Netspeak"—is more akin to the spoken word.

Computer-mediated communication (a fancy term for talking in chat rooms, via e-mail, or in online forums) fosters a kind of "secondary orality"—that is, a language that is "spoken" from the keyboard.[11] Visit any chat room, and you'll see secondary orality at work. The language of online Bible studies, such as the following chat room discussion of Philippians 1:6—"being confident of this very thing, that He who has begun a good work in you will complete it until the day of Jesus Christ" (NKJV)—has a distinctly casual "sound" to it:

```
<Heart4God> Paul is confident, not only of what
God has done "for" the readers in forgiving their
sins, . . .
<Heart4God> but also fo what he has done "IN" them.
<Heart4God> fo = for
<Acts_man> amen
<Heart4God> IN them. What does that mean to us?
<Acts_man> spiritual growth
<Nu_Thang> That salvation is just the beginning!
<Heart4God> GOOD!
<Nu_Thang> May I share a related verse?
<Heart4God> sure
<Nu_Thang> But we all, with open face beholding
as in a glass the *glory* of the Lord, are changed
into the same image from glory to glory, even as
by the Spirit of the Lord. <KJV 2 Cor. 3:18>
<Nu_Thang> He is making us like Him!!!!
<Acts_man> amen
<Heart4God> AMEN
<Heart4God> And that's the goal, eh?
<Nu_Thang> Yeppers
<Acts_man> :)[12]
```

Chat room ministries have the potential to reopen the book for many people who are unfamiliar with God's Word. Because chat happens in "real time," it turns the Net into a vehicle for immediate conversations. It is also highly interactive as well as highly "Net-oral."

Whereas literate cultures tend to be elitist, oral cultures "tend to be participatory and egalitarian," distributing "authority" throughout the community, writes Charles Ess, a professor of religion and philosophy at Drury University in Missouri.[13] The early Christian church was "an oral, more egalitarian culture" surrounded by the "literate, more hierarchical culture" of Greek and Jewish societies.[14] The language of the New Testament Scripture was in keeping with the early church's oral, egalitarian nature. As Eugene Peterson explains, the New Testament was written in the "street language" of its day, the "idiom of the playground and marketplace."[15]

Today, Netspeak is the language of our online agoras and virtual hangouts. Our efforts to communicate God's message to the online world must take into account the secondary orality of Net culture. We in the church must recognize that we no longer hold a privileged position in society. Our faith competes on a level playing field with every pseudo-religious group, every cult, and every other religion in the world. On the Net, we must relate the message of the gospel in a manner that reaches a culture that values diversity, tolerance, and equality.

Presenting the Bible in the language of the Net provides a more authentic experience for N-Geners, and if there's one thing the Net Generation values, it is authenticity. Teens are less interested in a "polished" presentation of the gospel than they are in "relevance, genuineness, and authenticity."[16] One reason so many young Christians are using the Internet to share the gospel is that they are not tied to the traditional, hierarchical structure of the modern-era church. We who are their elders could stand to learn from their examples.

Breathing Life into Bible-Bots

Perhaps one of the most "authentic" methods for communicating Scripture to N-Geners online is also one of the most automated and impersonal ways of doing it. The "bot"—short for robot—is the name that programmers have given to the software they create to manage chat rooms and electronic mailing lists and to perform other routine functions on the Net. As we saw in the introduction, a bot can be programmed to quote Scripture, adding immediacy and convenience to online Bible study. Through such Bible bots, the Word becomes software and dwells virtually among us in chat rooms, where Net-savvy Christians can easily share God's Word with someone in need of encouragement. As the Old Testament book of Proverbs tells us, "A word fitly spoken is like apples of gold in pictures of silver" (Prov. 25:11 KJV). How true this is in cyberspace, where a word fitly processed can accomplish great things.

Wyatt Houtz and Brandan Kraft, two young men who know the value of bots to share the gospel on the Net, saw an opportunity to build on that technology. In 1997, they created a "script," a kind of software code for chatters, called Christian Command, and it has become a popular tool for witnessing in Internet chat rooms. "Parables and spiritual warfare are at the click of a mouse tip," reads the promotional blurb on the Christian Command Web site (www.bornagain.net/cc). "Bible verses are available on demand. And peoples lives can be changed with the built in preaching that can aid as a witnessing tool."

These N-Gen entrepreneurs collaborated over the Net. Houtz was studying computer engineering and electrical engineering at Oakland University in Michigan. Kraft, a systems administrator in Webster Groves, Missouri, was a computer science student at the University of Missouri-Rolla. They worked with other friends on the Net who beta-tested the scripts, working together nonhierarchically and collaboratively to debug the software and improve it with each new release. As long as the church has devoted and talented cybersaints like Houtz and Kraft working to retell the story on the Net, there is hope for the church in cyberspace.

Hyper-Bibles

Turning Holy Scripture into holy hypertext makes Scripture more accessible in cyberspace. Hypertext documents are computerized pages that contain key words and phrases embedded with links to other hypertext documents, creating a nonlinear reading experience for readers. Hypertext has become the *lingua franca* of Web sites, CD-ROM software, and other computer applications. Most Bible software programs rely on hypertext to connect readers to related verses, concordances, commentaries, or other background information. Web sites such as the Bible Gateway (bible.gospelcom.net), which allows users to search several online Bible versions in a dozen different languages, make excellent use of the search and hypertext features of Bible CD software in the online environment. Several other online hyper-Bibles offer the same approach to retelling the good news to cyberculture. (The appendix of this book lists many of these sites.)

Writer and theologian Leonard Sweet hails hypertext as "the narrative mode and model of postmodern culture."[17] But not everyone welcomes its arrival with such enthusiasm. Christian philosopher and social critic Douglas Groothuis, for instance, warns that the hypertext's "malleable and movable" nature could render the traditional view of texts meaningless. Hypertext, Groothuis says, may threaten Scripture's status as unassailable and unchangeable. "This shift in emphasis dovetails with the postmodernist or deconstructionist attack on objective meaning, on the legitimacy of comprehensive worldviews, and on the integrity of literary texts as expressing the determined intention of their authors."[18] Quoting journalist Benjamin Woolley, Groothuis worries that hyperlinked communication in cyberspace, where Scriptures may be easily connected to other, less authoritative documents, images, sounds, and movies, "subverts the view, enshrined in the Bible, that books 'are written to be read in the order and fashion set out by the author.'"[19]

Charles Henderson, the organizing pastor for the First Church of Cyberspace (www.godweb.org), disagrees with these assertions. Hypertext "bears surprisingly close resemblance to the biblical text," Henderson writes, adding, "The worst possible approach to the Holy Scriptures is to read it in one uninterrupted, linear progression from start to finish. It is far preferable to wander in circular patterns in and around and through its varied poetry, history, saga, parable and story. As one does so, one finds that one passage plays itself off against another, though they were written hundreds of years apart by people who spoke entirely different languages. And as one threads a path through the text, one finds that its images and ideas emerge and play off against each other and against the situation in which one is living."[20]

Virtual Faith author Tom Beaudoin echoes Henderson's ideas about the Bible as a "hyper" document.

> When we read scripture, we click consciously or unconsciously on fragments of the text (we each have our own favorites), clicking mentally on a sermon we heard on this text, clicking on something a friend said, clicking on our last meal with that friend, clicking back on the text with a new perspective on it, clicking onto a book we read that gave us insight into this text, clicking on the friend that loaned us the book, clicking back on another scriptural text that reminds us of this concept and helps us understand it. It seems that our clothbound Bibles are already well versed in the ways of cyberspace.[21]

Although the Internet puts a virtual library of hypertext Bibles and study resources at the touch of a keystroke, we should proceed with caution. It is now easier than ever to string together snippets of Scripture without understanding their context or historical setting. As Groothuis explains, "Information retrieval is not synonymous with handling the truth wisely. Since computers cannot discern meaning, we cannot expect them to deliver wisdom. That is up to us, with God's help."[22]

Accessing God

The Internet is truly a liberating medium. Online hyper-Bibles—including those judiciously linked to extrabiblical resources, such as commentaries, articles, and video and audio clips—free Scripture from the confines of the page. Bible bots and chat resources such as Christian Command are to the Net Generation what the printing press was to Martin Luther and the Reformers: they're putting the Bible into the hands of the online masses. The Internet makes Scripture, and therefore God, more accessible to a generation that is alienated from traditional Christianity. It might be more appropriate to call online Christians "people of the bot" rather than "people of the Book." Chat room Bible studies, cyberscripture, and the many other online Christian resources are helping to spread the Word on the Net.

The availability of online Bibles and other religious writings signals a "virtual" return to the preliterate society at the time of Christianity's founding. Christian gatherings on the Internet bear more resemblance to the primitive church's house meetings than to the regimented weekly services of most Protestant denominations. Closely aligned to the broader postmodern movement for a more experiential faith—even though it might be considered only "virtually" experiential—the Christian presence in cyberspace can use the tools of the computer world to make God more real to those who seek Him.

In postmodern terms, the availability of online texts, religious or otherwise, provides "an experience of the eroding frontier between high and mass culture."[23] By making sacred texts accessible online, we not only make God more accessible but also tear down the boundaries between an elitist, literate culture (which many people believe the traditional church has become) and the egalitarian, "secondarily oral" culture of cyberspace (which is more similar to the early church than to the modern church). Information that was once held in the hands of an elite is now available to everyone who has the means to attain it. We break down the barriers between traditional church and the cyberchurch. In doing so, we are following a pattern set by Jesus Christ Himself, who, through His crucifixion, ripped away the temple veil that separated humanity from God (see Matt. 27:51; Eph. 2:14–16 KJV). By embracing the Net and its technology to share the powerful message of the Scriptures, the church again has the chance to tear away the veil that separates the postmodern world from the elitist modern church.

Of course, it is important that we use appropriately this newfound freedom to "access God." Merely trying to incorporate traditional modern Christianity into the postmodern, nonlinear world of cyberspace is doomed to failure. To put the new wine of postmodernism into our Enlightenment-era wineskins just won't work. As Jimmy Long notes in his book *Generating Hope,* the church that hopes to minister to postmodern people must emphasize the heart over the head and relational learning over cognitive, intellectual learning. "Bible study," Long adds, "needs to be more interactive and free-flowing."[24]

This point is true both on the Net and in "real life" church. An interactive, liquid, free-flowing approach with Scripture online can open doors for us to introduce the citizens of cyberspace to God and His Word. From this foundation, we can begin to make digital disciples through the creation of a new, vibrant form of community.

. . . .

eConnections: Online Resources for eMinistry

Bible, Thou Art Loosed!

Take a look at "The Unbound Bible" on the Web (unbound .biola.edu). How might such a resource make the Bible more accessible to an online culture that is more comfortable with pointing and clicking than with turning pages? How might "The Unbound Bible" be made even more Net-friendly?

A View of Jesus

Watch portions of the Jesus Film Project online at www.jesusfilm .org. How does this visual gospel square with the traditional text version? Does this video version translate well to the medium of cyberspace?

The Way of the Cross

This Good Friday (or any day), take in beliefnet's "Bitter Journey: The Way of the Cross" (www.beliefnet.com/story/21/story_2151_1.html), a multimedia presentation of Jesus' passion and death. For a slightly different perspective, experience another multimedia interpretation of the same event by Rated-G (www.rated-g.com/john316/).

The Bible Tells Me So

If you're wondering what the Bible says about a certain subject, go to "What the Bible Says" (wbsa.logos.com) and type a keyword into the search engine. You'll get a list of scriptural references linked to the full biblical text.

Secondary Orality

Read Professor Charles Ess's online article, "Prophetic Communities Online? Threat and Promise for the Church in Cyberspace" (www.drury.edu/faculty/ess/church/church.html). What do you make of this concept of "secondary orality"?

CHAPTER NINE

Virtual Community

Let us build ourselves a city.
—Genesis 11:4 NIV

ALL NEIGHBORHOODS HAVE their share of bullies. The chat rooms of cyberspace are no exception. For the Internet Relay Channel *#Church,* the bully was a teenage boy who went by the nickname PsyberDogg. He hounded the seekers and cybersaints who went to *#Church* for online fellowship. "I discovered a room called *#Church,*" he writes on his personal Web site, "so I figured I would anger them all by saying that I was Satan or the dread lord of all evil. Well, I did it and I was quickly banned." Chat room administrators often ban or "kick" people from a channel if they harass chatters or violate any of a channel's rules. "That became a routine, and for almost a week and a half, I would join *#Church* and anger people, and get kicked. Soon, whenever I got into the room, ops (channel operators) . . . would say, 'You come for your nightly kick/ban?'"

On one occasion, however, a channel operator began a private dialogue with this troubled teen. PsyberDogg warmed up to the channel op. He started visiting the room more often and became less belligerent. During one *#Church* chat, PsyberDogg committed his life to Christ.[1]

Through that experience, PsyberDogg encountered the living Christ in a virtual environment. But something else happened as well. PsyberDogg discovered the acceptance, love, and fellowship of a Christian community. That acceptance and love is what seekers should expect from the church. But would PsyberDogg's actions have been tolerated in a typical church meeting or youth group meeting? On the Net, where he could mouth off anonymously, and where boorish behavior is the norm, he was able to find compassion and hope. It was through the Net that he discovered true Christian community, and, as he later wrote on his Web site, those encounters with the members of *#Church* led him to find a church in his own, offline community.

More and more people seem to be searching for community these days, both on the Net and in the offline world. At the same time, community—in the sense of a "place," real or virtual, where one can find fellowship and a sense of belonging—is becoming harder to find. In our highly mobile culture, people are less likely to form lasting friendships. Even as people express a desire to build community, they seem to devote less time to traditional church activities.

According to pollster George Barna, the church in the United States has lost the ability to create and cultivate lasting communities because of Americans' transience, preference for variety, perception that "spiritual enlightenment comes from diligence in a discovery process," and "repositioning of religion as a commodity that we consume, rather than one in which we invest ourselves."[2] People are more inclined to "shop around" for a church that meets their needs. If one church doesn't meet all their needs, then they'll divide their allegiances and attend two or perhaps even three places of worship. Today's spiritual seekers appear to be more interested in a church's day care facilities and music than they are in the minister's theology or the church's heritage and traditions. Denominational "brand loyalty" is disappearing, even as a collective longing for a "direct experience of the divine"—"whether it's called the 'holy spirit' or 'cosmic consciousness' or the 'true self'"—is on the rise.[3]

If traditional church is perceived as being unable to meet the needs of the postmodern, tribal culture, then what about the Internet? Many people are searching for true community in cyberspace. Can the Internet, then, be of use to a church that seeks to create a sense of community that not only helps believers grow spiritually but also is open to those in need of Christ? Can the church truly reach out to the online world and establish a community in cyberspace?

Everywhere you turn on the Net, people are trying to "build us a city" in cyberspace. Some of the efforts are little more than modern-day towers of Babel, attempts to become as gods in cyberspace. Technopagans, extropians, and others see cyberspace as a kind of escape from the physical world. Others see the Internet as holding promise as a community of commerce. But for many others, Christian and non-Christian alike, the Internet is a community of a much broader sense: a place to play, to learn, to discuss and debate, to love, to live.

Those who turn to the Net in search of such community and a sense of belonging apparently aren't finding it in the "real world." This point is especially true for the Net Generation, which is spending quite a bit of time with modems whirring. The average teenager with an Internet connection spends more than twenty hours a week online, much of it in pursuit of community and relationships.[4] For many N-Geners, online relationships are as meaningful to them as their "real-world" relationships, often *more* meaningful.[5] Seeking connections that they aren't finding in their offline endeavors and growing up in a fragmented society where true community is becoming more and more scarce, these kids "long to belong" to a community. What they actually seek, "even without realizing it," writes Jimmy Long, "is the biblical community that God created us to be a part of."[6]

In *The Pearly Gates of Cyberspace,* Margaret Wertheim explains, "For young people especially, cyberspace beckons as a place where they might build a better 'life.'" The online world "may not be paradise," but "for an increasing number of America's youth cyberspace seems a more appealing place than the reality of their physical lives."[7]

As a space that is free from middle-class slump, and is immune from the problems of urban decay and social disintegration plaguing so many "real life" communities,
cyberspace beckons as a decidedly more utopian domain.
On the other side of the modem, these young men and
women see a space to meet and date in safety, a place where
they can have the kind of power and significance increasingly beyond reach in their physical lives.[8]

While philosophers and theologians debate whether any true
"community" can exist in cyberspace, teens are busy creating their
own virtual hangouts. For these N-Geners, the Net, in the words
of virtual community pioneer Howard Rheingold, seems to be
"one of the informal places where people can rebuild the aspects of
community that were lost when the malt shop became a mall."[9]

To be sure, these keyboard kids aren't hanging out at Pop's, the
malt shop venue of *Archie* comics fame. Their online refuges vary
from cybersex chat rooms to philosophy discussion forums. Sex,
music, and movies remain popular topics among this age group,
regardless of whether they're chatting online or at the local mall.
But don't sell the Net Generation short. They're also creating virtual venues to meet about more weighty matters. Artistic teens
and twentysomethings log on to Swanky (www.swanky.org), a virtual community of young graphic artists, to discuss their work,
swap homemade fonts and graphics, and share original poetry, essays, rants, and thoughts on various issues. Teenage computer nerds
by the thousands flock to sites like Slashdot (slashdot.org), where
they are accepted, rather than ridiculed, for their love of the Net
and computer games. Christian teens, too, are discovering a sense
of fellowship with like-minded followers at sites like The Coffee-
house (www.thecoffeehouse.com) and ChristianTeens (www
.christianteens.net). Individual church youth groups, as well as
parachurch youth ministries, augment their outreach to young
people with online community forums. Teen Mania (www
.teenmania.org), for example, hosts an active discussion forum for
young people who have participated in their "Acquire the Fire"

youth rallies. Live the Life Online (www.livethelife.org) was created as a place for teens who met at DC/LA Live the Life conferences to hook up with one another online.

In all of these virtual communities, kids are baring their souls. Discussions that would make a youth pastor cringe are frequent on Christian youth forums. Kids who feel like outcasts in their schools find solace on the Net. And young people aren't afraid to voice their opinions in the marketplace of ideas that is cyberspace. After the April 1999 massacre at Columbine High School in Littleton, Colorado, where two teenage boys gunned down a dozen classmates and a teacher, then killed themselves, teens poured out their thoughts in online forums. After Slashdot writer Jon Katz posted an article on the Columbine tragedy on Slashdot's Web site, teens who felt they were being harassed by school administrators because they wore trench coats (as did the two killers, members of a "trench coat mafia"), or played video games and surfed the Web, inundated Katz with electronic messages. "I got a steady stream of e-mail from middle and high school kids all over the country—especially from self-described oddballs," Katz writes. "Many of these kids saw themselves as targets of a new hunt for oddballs—suspects in a bizarre, systematic search for the strange and the alienated."[10] They shared their stories on other forums as well. "On Star Wars and X-Files mailing lists and websites and on AOL chat rooms and ICQ message boards, teenagers traded countless stories of being harassed, beaten, ostracized and ridiculed by teachers, students and administrators for dressing and thinking differently from the mainstream."[11]

The Net, it seems, is a world where teens of all stripes can share their thoughts without fear of repercussion.

But Is It "Real"?

Kids may find solace and a sense of community on the Net, but is this a good thing? Wouldn't it be better for them to go out and find community in their own schools, clubs, churches, and other "real-world" communities, rather than spending so much time at their computers, e-mailing and chatting with faceless, anonymous "friends"? Several critics of the Internet—Douglas Groothuis, Clifford Stoll, and Neil Postman among them—raise some legitimate concerns about the nature of virtual communities. They are skeptical that an online gathering constitutes a community at all. Groothuis, for instance, says that the very idea of virtual community "challenges the very meaning of community and the nature of our sociality."[12] He adds, "Generally speaking, the kind of community required for the resuscitation of national life requires the grace that comes through the human touch, the human voice, the human gaze." Cyberspace "can only mimic or mirror these things (however convincingly); it cannot create them."[13]

Clifford Stoll, the author of *Silicon Snake Oil,* holds similar notions about the nature of community online. He claims that "only the 'illusion' of community is created via CMC (computer-mediated communication), that the only relationships created are 'shallow, impersonal, and often hostile.'"[14]

Such arguments assume that "community" is bound by geography and physical human interaction. In cyberspace, communities are most likely to develop among people with common interests or beliefs, rather than geographically. The Net is also changing the way we look at friendship and, consequently, fellowship. As Brittney G. Chenault points out in a research article, Stoll "assumes that to make and have 'friends,' you must interact in 'real life.' . . . The assumption, however, that Stoll makes is that interacting with participants in CMC is not 'really' interacting with 'people.'"[15] For many N-Geners, however, online interaction is as real as face-to-face interaction.

The Internet is not the first technology to challenge our concept of community. The printing press, for instance, radically redefined community in medieval society and played an important role in the shift from a premodern to modernist outlook in Europe. The advent of this new communications technology "destroyed oral tradition and thus sabotaged the local community," writes Mark Galli, an editor for *Computing Today.* "No longer did children depend on parents or town elders to pass on local stories or traditions, to interpret life, or to form their character. When books became readily available, the whole world—with its myriad of traditions and stories and values—could be consulted, and the role of family and community diminished."[16] The printing press also gave rise to a new kind of community: the university. In much the same way, computers and the Internet are giving rise to new notions about community, if not to new forms of community itself.

For a growing number of Christians, cybercommunities *are* as real as flesh-and-blood fellowship. One member of an electronic discussion list about the writer C. S. Lewis says that the list was "the closest thing I had to a steady Christian community" while he was between churches. He adds, "Many members of the group are my friends, even if I never meet them face to face in this life."[17] In *E-vangelism: Sharing the Gospel in Cyberspace,* I wrote of a Mauritanian woman living in Shanghai, China, who signed up for an online prayer ministry that was her main connection to other Christians because of restrictions in China. In her opinion, any discussion about whether virtual communities are "real" was a moot point.[18]

Gen-X writer Tom Beaudoin claims that cybercommunities "can be as bonded as some physical communities and are therefore no less 'real.'"[19] In fact, Beaudoin asserts, "Dedication to a religious cyber community can be as gratifying and important as allegiance to any 'real' religious institution."[20]

Perhaps that's why so many teens are gathering online to talk about everything from dating to politics. Many of them are engaging in "church" discussions without realizing it. According to the Barna Research Group, "A substantial number of cyberchatters engage in dialogue related to faith, spirituality, religion, meaning and truth—the very types of conversations that are often initiated or fostered by churches. Teens do not think of those conversations as religious expression, but the sense of community and the spiritual beliefs fostered by such dialogue on spiritual matters is identical to what the traditional church seeks to create within its congregation."[21]

The Real and the Virtual

Little doubt exists that new virtual "congregations" are being created outside the walls of the traditional church. Christians are meeting in chat rooms to worship. They're discussing theology over e-mail. They're sharing prayer requests over the Internet. But does this mean they are leaving their real-world spiritual communities for the virtual? On the contrary, their involvement in online communities is strengthening their offline spiritual lives. In her studies of an online Christian community, Heidi Campbell found that most members of that group saw the virtual community as a supplement to their local church. The online group "filled in gaps in teaching and ministry unavailable to them" and also provided a network of support and encouragement the members find lacking in their local congregations. Campbell also found that participation in the online community helped broaden the perspectives of many Christians, "exposing them not just to information, but to 'brothers and sisters' from all over the world."[22]

Christian teens, too, see the Net as something that augments their offline Christian experiences, rather than something that replaces them. In a survey of sixty-four N-Geners who are part of online communities aimed at Christian teens, fully 100 percent claimed that they were either "just as involved" or "more involved" in their churches since getting on the Net.[23] Exactly how involved these N-Geners were before logging on, however, is unknown. If their church involvement was similar to that of the average church-goer, then the church has other issues to worry about besides their Internet use.

Seemingly, concerns about the Net replacing the church might be unfounded. Nevertheless, it is vital that we understand the role of virtual community in relation to the "real" community of the church. If Augustine's words are true that community is "nothing else than a harmonious collection of individuals,"[24] then it seems that an online gathering, if harmonious, would be just as much a community as a Sunday morning church service. Cybersaints should feel as comfortable in a real-world church setting as they are seated before their computer monitor. Church and parachurch organizations should see cyberspace and virtual communities as things that augment, but do not replace, real community.[25]

Yet, some discord remains between traditional churches and ministries that fear the free-flowing nature of cyberspace and the Net-savvy teens who are suspicious of highly structured institutions such as "the church." People in the church who can work to develop a stronger tie between the "real" Christian community of the local church and the "virtual" yet global Christian community of online believers will find themselves in a very important position of ministry as the Internet continues to grow in importance and influence. Creating a more "seamless" community—one that unites the real and the virtual—can only strengthen the church. What is needed, writes Heidi Campbell, "is a balance between on-line and real world community involvement" and a recognition of "the strengths and weaknesses inherent in both."[26] We in the church must come to the understanding that the virtual community "is not a mythic land of milk and honey, but neither is it any more dangerous, hostile, or unwelcoming than 'real life.'"[27]

"By God's design," writes Mark Galli, "people can't live without community any more than they can live without breathing. And though this new technology will continue to transform our communities, it will never thwart people from forming new ones."[28]

The church's role in the future of cyberspace is critical. The community of Christianity must grow strong on the Internet because, as Leonard Sweet explains, the church "is the only community on earth that can confront the evil one. For it is the only community on earth to whom the keys of the kingdom were given."[29] On the Internet, the church must develop communities for our children that are safe, loving, and based on the biblical model of fellowship and worship. No reason exists today for a church *not* to be present on the World Wide Web. Free Web space is available from a plethora of Internet services. But establishing a presence is not enough. Use a church Web site as a launching pad to reach the Net Generation. Create a chat room on the church's site or an electronic mailing list. Establish a Web ministry team to monitor the chat room and to send out e-mail to the congregation. Involve your church's teens in the process. In fact, why not let the teens lead the project? They're the ones who know the medium best anyway.

The church must move beyond developing a presence in cyberspace, however. Christians must populate cybercommunities—chat rooms, Web-based communities, online forums, and other models of virtual gathering places—to be the salt and light that the dark reaches of the Net so desperately need. Through new communities in this new medium, we can begin to retell the old, old story that they may discover Jesus in a new way.

. . . .

eConnections: Online Resources for eMinistry

A Cybercommunity Classic

Howard Rheingold's 1993 book *The Virtual Community* is considered a classic study on Internet community. Read excerpts of the book online at www.rheingold.com/vc/book/. More of Rheingold's writings are accessible from his main Web site (www.rheingold.com).

Finding a Home on the Net

Do some exploring of virtual community on the Net. A good first stop might be Deja.com's Usenet Service (www.deja.com/usenet/) or Tile.Net (tile.net). These searchable catalogs can lead you to Internet forums on any topic under the sun. For communities specific to Christianity, visit the Internet for Christians directory, "Christian Email Mailing Lists" (www.gospelcom.net/ifc/mail/view/).

Build Your Own Community

If you're interested in starting an online community of your own, read the Online Community Toolkit (www.fullcirc.com/community/communitymanual.htm) for helpful tips to get you started.

Give Life to Your List

Read "The Life Cycle of a Discussion List" (wdvl.internet.com/ Internet/Email/life_cycle.html) for more tips on creating list-based communities.

Spiritual Typecasting

Are you a hardcore skeptic? Spiritual dabbler? A confident believer? An old-fashioned seeker? The beliefnet Web community (www.beliefnet.com) can help you define your "spiritual type" through a twenty-five-question quiz. Take the quiz at www.beliefnet .com/resource1.html, and then join one of beliefnet's many discussion groups to talk about your spirituality.

CHAPTER TEN

Cyber Stories

And these words which I command you today shall be in your heart. You shall teach them diligently to your children, and shall talk of them when you sit in your house, when you walk by the way, when you lie down, and when you rise up.

—Deuteronomy 6:6–7 NKJV

HE IS NOW A YOUNG MAN in his twenties. But it wasn't long ago that he was struggling with a problem familiar to many N-Geners. "I was 11 years old when my parents divorced," he writes in an online testimony. "And as my dad moved out, I felt empty because I knew we were not going to spend as much time together like we used to." Despite the split-up, the young man managed to build a strong relationship with his father.

A few years later, however, another tragedy struck. "I remember the day my father told me he had AIDS." The news, he writes, came "like an unexpected blow to the face." He was fourteen when his father told him. The young man became withdrawn and sad. "Little by little, my heart grew cold to everyone except my dad." Watching his father waste away, he prepared for the worst. During his father's last week of life, the young man explains, a family member shared Christ with his father. As soon as his father ended the prayer, "he said that he saw several men dressed in white saying that they were going to stay with him until he went home. I couldn't understand then, but now I believe they were angels sent by God."

The young man's story ends on this note of hope for teens who have seen AIDS devastate their loved ones. "AIDS is a deadly disease that affects everybody—not just the one infected. I went through a lot of emotional distress when my father passed away, but through God's help, I once again feel joy. If anyone reading this is infected with the HIV virus or knows someone that is, my advice to you is to pray to God to give you comfort, peace, and joy. I guarantee he will."

The young man's testimony is one of many woven throughout a Web site called Hopenet (www.hopenet.net). The site's real-life testimonies also contain hyperlinks to relevant passages from a Web-based version of The Book of Hope, which is a harmony of the gospels. The Hopenet site is a virtual community for teens, with chat rooms, discussion boards, and an online game designed to help teens learn to make good decisions along the road of life.

But the key to Hopenet's appeal is its stories: stories written by young people for young people; stories about divorce, peer pressure, broken friendships, and broken hearts; stories with which teens can relate.

This Is My Story, This Is My Song

In every culture throughout history, storytelling has been the key means of passing timeless truths from generation to generation. Our Christian faith springs from one of the greatest story-telling traditions in history—that of the Jewish people. In Deuteronomy, God commanded the Jews to retell the stories of deliverance and miraculous events again and again to their children. God told them to tell the stories always, "whether you're at home or walking along the road or going to bed at night, or getting up in the morning" (Deut. 6:6–7 CEV).

Throughout the history of Christianity, telling the story of Jesus has been an important method for sharing the faith. At the heart of Christianity's two great holidays—Christmas and Easter— are two of the most compelling tales of our culture. To rediscover the power of the story of Christ's birth, one need only attend a children's Christmas pageant. Watch the little boys in the oversized bathrobes playing the role of the shepherds. See the little girl in her white sheet, the curly-haired, freckle-faced angel of the Lord, her voice quavering as she recites those famous lines from the gospel of Luke: "Fear not: for, behold, I bring you good tidings of great joy, which shall be to all people. For unto you is born this day in the city of David a Saviour, which is Christ the Lord" (Luke 2:10–11 KJV). Or attend a church choir's performance of Handel's *Messiah* and hear the story set to music. Attend a passion play and experience again the power of the greatest story ever told.

The gospel message is drama. It is poetry. It is music. It is story.

Somewhere along the line, however, the church turned away from the power of story and settled for discourse, debate, and linear, rational argument. We relegated our pageantry and storytelling to Christmas and Easter, and then we asked ourselves why so many nominal Christians managed to find their way into our sanctuaries on only those two holidays. The church has such a marvelous story to tell. So why aren't we telling it more? If "the future belongs to the 'storytellers,'" as theologian Leonard Sweet claims,[1] then why is the church so hesitant to embrace the ministry of storytelling?

For too long we've emphasized the rational, the systematic, the "head" and not the "heart." To reach postmodern N-Geners, the church must tell its story, and the Internet is an ideal medium for storytelling. It is a medium that is well suited for the preacher who desires to use words not only "to explain, expound, exhort," but also to "evoke, to set us dreaming as well as thinking, to use words as at their most prophetic and truthful," and "not only try to give answers to the questions that we ask or ought to ask but which help us to hear the questions that we do not have words for asking."[2]

Somebody Testify

Testimonials are a time-honored means of witnessing in any medium. From Pentecostal "testimony meetings" to conversion stories on personal Web sites, "Testimony to our firsthand experience of Christ's grace oft times is more powerful than logic."[3] Whereas reasoning focuses "more on objective truth or doctrine," story in the form of testimony "relates to personal, subjective experience."[4]

Lyndell Enns, director of the Momentum program of Campus Crusade for Christ Canada (CCCC), knows all about the power of personal testimony. The personal testimonies of both the famous and the not-so-famous drive CCCC's "Power to Change" Web site (www.powertochange.com). "If we're honest," begins the text on this seeker-friendly Web site, "most of us would have to admit there's something we'd like to change in our life. Maybe it's our job, the quality of our relationships, or even our outlook on life. . . . But how?"[5] The site then leads readers to a variety of true-life testimonies about how people of all stripes overcame life's challenges through Jesus Christ.

The authors of the stories include some famous names, such as tennis star Michael Chang and former coach of the Washington Redskins pro football team Joe Gibbs. But it also includes the testimonies of everyday Christians, including N-Gener Stephen Nielsen. "My life was off to a bad start," Nielsen begins. In just a few paragraphs, the young man recounts his struggles with attention deficit disorder, flunking the eighth grade, and dealing with put-downs from classmates—issues with which many teens can relate—and presents how accepting Jesus Christ as his Savior changed his perspective. "I started seeing those who laughed at me as people, instead of focusing on the hurtful words they were saying. And I found out I could love them."

Beyond Logic

Like so many others in the ministry, pastor and author David Fisher was accustomed to taking the logical approach to preaching without considering the interests of the audience. But a meeting with a group of young skeptics showed him just how much more powerful a good story can be. Before his first meeting with the group, Fisher prepared his traditional, straightforward presentation. He developed his usual airtight, rational, scriptural case for the divinity of Christ and methodically presented the case to this jury of young skeptics. "The audience was polite but very restrained and apparently not very impressed," he recalls. A week later, he decided to take a different approach. "I talked about the church and told stories of the power of the gospel I have seen and experienced myself over the years. The discussion afterward was electric. These young skeptics were very interested in a community of faith that demonstrated the grace and power of God."[6]

One older skeptic—a skeptic of the Internet, anyway—is Andrew M. Greeley, the Roman Catholic priest, sociologist, and best-selling novelist who is better known for telling stories of fiction. Greeley's Web site of homilies (www.agreeley.com) is gaining an online following that rivals the readership of all of his nonfiction works combined. With the care of a master storyteller, Greeley now crafts his online homilies to perfection, cognizant that "through them I may be preaching to more people on a single Sunday than I have in all the other Sundays of my life put together."[7]

The lessons that Fisher and Greeley have learned about communicating the gospel in new ways and through new media reinforce the power of story. Leonard Sweet, a firm believer that no one should exit seminary without a thorough command of the Bible stories, also recognizes the importance of preaching the gospel through story.

Jesus' life was not an essay. Jesus' life was not a doctrine. Jesus' life was not a sermon. Jesus' life was a story. People don't live essays or doctrines or sermons. They live stories. People are not pulled from the edge of the pit by essays or doctrines or sermons. They are rescued by stories. They are healed by stories.[8]

"The Christian message," Sweet continues, "is not a timeless set of moral principles or a code of metaphysics. The Christian message is a story, the greatest story ever told, of love come down from heaven to earth, a love so vast and victorious that even hatred could not keep it down."[9]

Unfortunately, few young people know the power of that story. They aren't hearing it in church. Even if it's being told, they aren't hearing it if it is being told irrelevantly, couched in theological terms, or presented in thirty-minute lectures. That is why Todd Hahn and David Verhaagen, writing about Generation X, urge churches to begin "telling the old story in new ways" to reach a generation that has no story of its own.[10] "To reach our generation," they write, "we must dare to tell good stories for the sake of the stories, refusing to compromise on beauty or tension or any of the elements that make a story a real story. If we have a good grasp of Christian truth and if we are loving God and people, our stories, like (C. S.) Lewis's and (J. R. R.) Tolkien's, will warm cold hearts, thaw frozen minds, and change lives."[11]

The Narrative on the Net

We might not all write like C. S. Lewis or J. R. R. Tolkien, but we all have a story to tell. To share the gospel with seekers on the Net effectively, we must make the gospel story "our" story. A generation that craves authenticity and experience does not want to read rehashed Bible stories but stories of how God is real in our lives. Our witness to cyberspace must resonate with the truth of the gospel, as well as the truth of our own experience. Incorporating the power of story into our witness—what Jimmy Long calls "narrative evangelism"—is an effective approach for reaching postmoderns. "Narrative evangelism," Long writes, "merges 'our story' with 'God's story' through sharing it with others. Narrative evangelism is preferred in a postmodern context."[12]

That's the foundation of the gospel message—the story of God's divine intervention into the lives of humanity. After all, isn't Jesus Christ's descent into this world—of God's becoming flesh and dwelling among us (John 1:14 KJV)—nothing more and nothing less than the tale of God's story merging with our story? Similarly, the New Testament writings of the apostles, from the Gospels to Paul's letters, all bear witness to God's story merging with those of the authors.

A Christian teen named Katie has posted a testimony on the Web site of Mililani Baptist Church in Mililani, Hawaii, that beautifully illustrates how God's story can merge with ours.

> It was 6:26 P.M. sharp!, the time for our Tuesday night youth worship service at Mililani Baptist Church. It started off as a regular service—we sang praises to God and watched the drama team perform a skit. I looked around and the service was packed with teenagers. I never imagined that in that next hour, I would completely turn my life around and shape who I now am and what I stand for.
>
> It all began when the drama team left the stage, and my youth pastor began his sermon. He was preaching on a passage in Revelations which states, "So because you are lukewarm, and neither hot nor cold, I will spit you out of my mouth (Revelation 3:16 NAS)." I realized that I believed in Christ Jesus, but that I was lukewarm in my faith. A swear word would come out of my mouth every once in a while, most of my friends were not Christians, and I was ashamed to tell people about my relationship with Jesus. I had never surrendered my whole life to Him. I knew that I could no longer go on with my life unless Christ was my top priority. I wanted to be glorifying Him in all of my thoughts, words, and actions.
>
> My mind was set and I was ready to make my promise to God and myself that I would do my best to follow the Holy Bible daily and the examples Jesus set for us while He was here on earth. I went up to the front of the sanctuary, and kneeled at the alter. I prayed that the Lord would help me keep my promise for all of eternity.[13]

God calls upon us to "testify" of His power in our lives. Jesus' command to "Go into all the world and preach the gospel to every creature" (Mark 16:14 NKJV) carries with it the implicit command to tell the story, to merge God's story with our own. On the Net, we can share our testimonies in many ways. Telling our story through interactive chat, either in chat rooms or through one-on-one conversations (through instant messaging systems such as ICQ or personal direct chat with people on chat channels), gives us the chance to carry on a dialogue in real time. But sharing your testimony via chat is best done one-to-one outside of a crowded chat room, where your message is liable to get lost in the "noise" of other simultaneous conversations. It also is possible to share testimonies through online forums, such as Usenet newsgroups. But to avoid the wrath and flames of fellow newsgroup users, such sharing is probably best done in response to another writer's request for help rather than as a general posting to the newsgroup. Responding to someone's request for prayer, for instance, with a brief testimony of how God answered your prayer in a similar circumstance, is a better approach than posting your testimony with no connection to other topics being discussed in the forum.

Perhaps the best way to share your testimony on the Internet is by posting it on a personal Web site. By doing so, you are presenting a consistent message to everyone you share the testimony with—those who surf to your site, as well as those you meet in chat rooms or online forums that you refer to your site. Although the Web is a passive medium, which means that people have to take the initiative to visit your site to read your message, it is perhaps best suited to telling the story. And just because it is passive does not mean that a Web site cannot be interactive. At the Hopenet Web site, for instance, N-Geners can discover Web-based chat rooms as well as effective stories that deal with some of the things that concern teens most—such as loneliness, alienation, family life, and peer pressure. Other N-Gen-oriented Web sites include links to music, video, games, chat, and virtual postcards.

Tips for Testimonies

Perhaps you feel unqualified to write a testimony for the Web. When it comes to writing, you're no Andrew Greeley. Or you're afraid that your words will ring hollow or seem trite on the screen. Campus Crusade for Christ International has developed a Web site to help people write their testimonies with the aid of the Net. Called "5 Clicks to Sharing Your Faith," the Web site is an interactive teaching aid based on study materials found in Campus Crusade founder Bill Bright's book on personal evangelism, *5 Steps to Sharing Your Faith*. The Web site takes users through a step-by-step approach to writing their personal testimonies and includes tips on what *not* to say when sharing Christ with a nonbeliever. Upon completion of the online "training," users are asked to identify three people they wish to see come to Christ, and they are then urged to contact WorldChangers to receive ten free copies of the pamphlet *The Four Spiritual Laws* to share while witnessing.[14]

Whether you follow the "5 Clicks" approach or prefer to write your story without the aid of the Net, the following tips for writing effective testimonies can help.

- *Be honest.* Don't distort the details and facts of your story. There is no need to sensationalize your testimony in an attempt to make it more exciting. Remember, N-Geners are looking for authenticity, and many of them are sophisticated enough to spot a phony, even on the Web.
- *Emphasize the power of grace, not the power of sin.* "At times," writes Eric Elder of an online ministry called The Ranch (theranch.org), "it may be necessary to share some details of sin to show the power of God. But please do not bring unnecessary attention to elements that are already much too glorified in the world."
- *Include biblical references that will point people back to Scripture.* "A living testimony that sheds light on the living Word draws people further into their own search of the Scriptures for answers."[15]

More Than Just a Story

Narrative evangelism—telling the story of God through our own personal stories—will continue to be an important component of the church's emphasis on digital discipleship as we minister to the residents of cyberspace. Yet, we should not get so wrapped up in storytelling that we forget to relate our story to the truth of the Scriptures. "We can never forget," write Todd Hahn and David Verhaagen, "that the gospel really is propositional truth that must be either accepted or rejected."[16]

As we spin our tales in the Web of cyberspace, let us always remember that the goal is not merely to tell a good tale, but to draw people to Christ.

- -

eConnections: Online Resources for eMinistry

Change Agents

Visit the Power to Change Web site (www.powertochange.com) or Stonewall Revisited (www.stonewallrevisited.com) and read some of the testimonies on these sites. Are these personal stories effective bridges to the Net Generation?

Journey Among the Journals

Remember keeping a daily or weekly journal as a teen? Today's N-Geners keep their journals online for all to see. They write about movies, music, work, the mundane, God, spirituality, and just about anything else. Visit the Journal Ring (www.baddgrrl.com/JournalRing.htm) to read some random entries. Or for a more comprehensive list, go to the Yahoo! directory of personal journals (dir.yahoo.com/Social_Science/Communications/Writing/Journals_and_Diaries/Individual_Journals_and_Diaries/Online).

Plumb Bobs, Patched Teddy Bears, and DNA

Check out these three short bits of Internet writing: "What's a Plumb Bob?" by Eric Elder (101sites.com/whatsaplumbbob.htm); "On Patches and Bears," a poem by Lois Turley (www.carenurse .com/bears/about.html); and "DNA, the Jewish Priesthood and the End of Organized Religion," by John Miller (www.chapel42.com/ dna/index.htm). How do the authors employ their own experiences and interests in their writings to merge their narratives with the meta-narrative of Christianity? In other words, how do *their* stories become one with *God's* story?

Art and the Church

Read "A Letter to Artists," from Pope John Paul II, at the *Re:- generation Quarterly* Web site (www.regenerator.com/5.4/letter .html). "Art," John Paul writes, "has a unique capacity to take one or other facet of the message and translate it into colors, shapes and sounds which nourish the intuition of those who look or listen. It does so without emptying the message itself of its transcendent value and its aura of mystery. The Church has need especially of those who can do this on the literary and figurative level, using the endless possibilities of images and their symbolic force." How can the church's artists use the medium of cyberspace to communicate Jesus?

CHAPTER ELEVEN

Worldwide Witness

And this gospel of the kingdom will be preached in all
the world as a witness to all the nations.
                                                —Matthew 24:14 NKJV

EVERY SUMMER SINCE 1990, thousands of people have poured into southern California sports stadia—not to watch the Dodgers, Padres, or Angels play baseball, but to hear Greg Laurie proclaim the gospel. One of the most dynamic crusade evangelists since Billy Graham, Laurie's annual Harvest Crusade is a flashy event. It looks more like a rock festival than a traditional evangelistic crusade. That atmosphere draws many young people who might not otherwise respond to God's call. The final two nights of the four-night crusade is tailored to attract Southern California's youth culture. Superstar Christian bands such as Audio Adrenaline, Big Tent Revival, the Kry, and the Orange County Supertones draw a young crowd to those Friday and Saturday night meetings.

On the final night of Laurie's 1998 crusade, a crowd of fifty-three thousand—mostly teens and young adults—packed Disney's Edison Field in Anaheim, California, while four thousand more gathered in the parking lot to watch the events unfold on a Jumbo-Tron screen. But Laurie's audience wasn't limited to the packed stadium or the overflow crowd in the parking lot. For the second consecutive year, his preaching was also broadcast live over the Internet. Through RealAudio and RealVideo, two online technologies that allow digital bits of sight and sound to "stream" through cyberspace, Laurie's preaching actually went out to all the world. At least one person—someone tuning in from Japan—made a commitment to Christ thanks to the cybercast.[1] A year earlier, a gang member in New York City also committed his life to Jesus after tuning in to the online version of the Harvest Crusade.[2] Even after the summer Harvest Crusades are over, the ministry's Internet outreach continues. According to Harvest Crusade officials, about a dozen people a week receive Christ after watching a video presentation of the gospel on Harvest's Web site (www.harvest.org).[3]

Elsewhere on the Net, dozens more are receiving Christ via Web sites of other ministries. Some are big operations, along the lines of the Harvest Crusade. (Prior to the 2000 crusades, volunteers in Laurie's ministry went "door-to-door" in chat rooms, inviting surfers to tune in to the crusade's cybercasts.)[4] Others are small, one-person operations. People are also encountering Christ in Internet chat rooms, through discussions on various Internet forums, and through one-on-one e-mail correspondence with Christians, Christian counselors, online pastors and chaplains, or other ministers. Christians by the thousands are sharing the gospel online, and cyberseekers are responding.

Many of the most savvy online "e-vangelists"[5] are members of the Net Generation cyberchurch. Wyatt Houtz and Brandan Kraft, the entrepreneurial cybersaints who created the Christian Command chat script discussed in chapter 8, are prime examples of N-Geners who are using computer and Internet technology to help the church be salt and light in cyberspace. From the Net's earliest days, individual Christians, more than the institutional church, have been the most active and aggressive Internet evangelists. One reason for that fact has to do solely with demographics. College professors and students were among the first to gain access to the online world, and many Christian graduate students contended for the faith on Usenet newsgroups such as *soc.religion.christian* long before the church established a significant presence online. Even after churches and ministries got on the Net, ministry leaders remained skeptical of the new technology or were ignorant of its value as a tool for sharing God's message of hope in a cyberculture that many people see as hopeless.

Individual Christians continue to advance the gospel message in cyberspace more visibly than does the institutional church. Today, N-Geners are becoming "fishers of men" on the Net, using chat rooms and instant messaging to share Christ with their virtual buddies.

But traditional churches and Christian organizations are finally catching on and catching up. Saving souls in cyberspace was the focus of a conference that brought together dozens of the world's biggest ministry organizations. The Internet Evangelism Conference (www.webevangelism.org), first held in a suburb of Chicago in April 1999, drew representatives from more than ninety organizations— from megaministries such as Campus Crusade for Christ International (www.ccci.org) and the Billy Graham Evangelistic Association (www.bgea.org) to one-person Internet outreaches such as Peggie's Place (www.gospelcom.net/peggiesplace) and Eric Elder Ministries (theranch.org), as well as Christian universities and major evangelical denominations. A second conference was held in Orlando, Florida, in November 2000. This mixture of ministries, working together toward a common goal, is a hopeful sign that ministries both large and small are ready to take a more assertive approach to evangelism on the Internet.

The Great Commission Mission

Regardless of what various ministries are doing with the Net, Jesus' mandate to the church remains clear and unchanged through the centuries, regardless of whether we get online. Christ calls us, the church, to "make disciples of all the nations" (Matt. 28:19 NKJV). After nearly two thousand years of Christian outreach, we have a chance to fulfill the Great Commission mandate to make disciples in a new way, through this new medium of the Internet.

We also have the chance to reach a new "people group"[6]—the Netizens of cyberspace.

The Net gives us, as online-witnessing Christians, an opportunity to get back to our New Testament roots of evangelism: meeting real people a few at a time and establishing meaningful, personal relationships with them. Building relationships is the New Testament model for evangelism, and this approach resonates with the Net Generation. N-Geners seek community and relationships online. Their thirst for connecting person-to-person presents us with a tremendous opportunity to introduce them to the community of faith.

Adapting the early church's model of evangelism to the Net is an ideal way to reach N-Geners. Even though the Internet is the newest communications medium, it uniquely facilitates the personal, one-to-one approach that the first Christians favored. As pastor, evangelist, and missionary Tom Stebbins notes, the majority of early Christians were influenced by the people in their "networks of trust relationships," in which the gospel is presented by someone whom the person already knows and trusts.[7] Using this approach, one can share the gospel in an unhurried manner, and the witness's lifestyle, already known to the nonbeliever, adds credibility to the message.[8]

Jesus called this approach "making disciples." Today, it's often called "friendship evangelism," "lifestyle evangelism" or "relationship evangelism." Regardless of the name, however, it is Jesus' original plan to reach the entire world with the message of salvation, and it is based on the efforts of ordinary Christians. Each of us is called to build relationships with nonbelievers, work to develop those relationships into friendships, create a level of trust with these nonbelieving friends, and then present the gospel message to them at the appropriate time. It's a time-tested, God-inspired method that works on the job, in the home, with family members and friends, and with acquaintances. It also works in the world of cyberspace.

E-vangelism: Building Friendships Online

As we've already seen, the Internet is teeming with people who are looking for meaningful relationships. The popularity of chat rooms devoted to stimulating relationships—everything from legitimate friendships to cybersex encounters—is evidence of this hunger for community. Many of those online seekers are members of the Net Generation.

For the church, the Internet is a truly global opportunity to share Christ, a mission field that is ripe for the harvest. Now is the time to go out into that field. To paraphrase Paul's words to Timothy, Christians who are going online must do the work of an "e-vangelist"— an electronic evangelist (see 2 Tim. 4:5 NKJV).

Electronic evangelism is relationship evangelism via the Internet. It is meeting people online, building community, and developing real relationships with them. But one very real problem keeps the cyberchurch from doing much e-vangelism, and it is a problem that has its roots in the "real world" church. A majority of Christians, whether online or in the pew, do not want to leave the comfort zones of the Christian community. In Western culture, the average Christian is taught to keep untainted from the secular world. The result is an insulation from the people to whom we're supposed to be telling the gospel of Jesus Christ. We spend more time reading Christian books, listening to Christian music, watching Christian programming, attending church-sponsored events, and surrounding ourselves with fellow Christians than we do being "salt and light" in our communities. Similarly, the typical cybersaint spends much of his or her online time in "Christian-friendly" environments. We visit Christian chat rooms; surf to Christian Web sites; read online articles written by Christian authors for a Christian audience; download Christian music to play on our multimedia computers; correspond electronically with Christian friends; and subscribe to Christian e-mail lists that provide us with daily meditations, Bible studies, and other inspirational messages.

Nothing is wrong with any of these actions. The Net includes many exceptional resources to help a Christian grow spiritually. But if we are serious about seeing the lost on the Internet come into the kingdom, then we must go to where they are.

Approaches to Net Evangelism

Christian author Joe Aldrich writes about the three approaches to personal evangelism: proclamational (preaching the gospel), confrontational/intrusional (going on "sorties" into enemy territory, such as bars; conducting door-to-door campaigns; or passing out tracts on street corners), and incarnational/relational (the "lifestyle" approach to evangelism).[9] Although all three of these approaches have merit and can be used successfully to win the lost to Christ, most of us are best suited to adopt the third approach. Not many of us are called to be proclamational evangelists—in the manner of Billy Graham or Greg Laurie, for example—and the confrontational/intrusional approach, although frequently emphasized in church soul-winning classes, all too often backfires. (As Aldrich notes, a zealous but insensitive person trying to witness in the confrontational style can push a person farther away from Christ.)[10] That leaves lifestyle evangelism, an approach that can work as well on the Net as it does in the workplace or at school.

The proclamational and confrontational methods both center on the spoken word—and it is important for all Christians to know *what* to say and *when* to say it. Scripture says that we should "always be ready to give a defense to everyone who asks you a reason for the hope that is in you" (1 Peter 3:15 NKJV). In cyberspace, where people are judged more on their ability to argue persuasively than on their appearance, the written word can be especially powerful. Lifestyle evangelism, however, emphasizes witnessing through relationships and letting our lifestyles be the "Word incarnate."

The lifestyle evangelism approach is firmly rooted in Scripture. Writing to the Corinthian church, Paul says that the believer is "an epistle of Christ, ministered by us, written not with ink but by the Spirit of the living God, not on tablets of stone but on tablets of flesh, that is, of the heart" (2 Cor. 3:3 NKJV). Our lives, therefore, are to be epistles—God's love letters to the world. Jesus Himself calls believers "the salt of the earth" and "the light of the world" (Matt. 5:13–14 NKJV), and tells us, "Let your light so shine before men, that they may see your good works and glorify your Father in heaven" (v. 16 NKJV).

A lifestyle witness allows people to see how God works in our lives. Our challenge in cyberspace, then, is to let the people who are on the Net see the good works in our lives and to let those good works direct them to God. Because our lives on the Net are "virtual" lives, we face new challenges in witnessing with our lifestyles online. But these challenges can be met effectively if we take the proper approach and understand the culture in which we are called to witness.

In an online world that is increasingly postmodern, evangelism that focuses on building relationships will be more effective, especially when viewed in the context of a community. We must be prepared *first* to invest more time in creating a sense of community online and then to welcome seekers into our online communities. From there, we can focus more on sharing Christ with the new "community convert." Jimmy Long explains, "Many people with a postmodern mind-set experience a two-stage conversion. First, the person becomes converted to the community, which may be a small group or a larger community. Over a period of time the seeker begins to identify with the community and feels a sense of belonging. At this point the seeker may be a member of the community without having made a commitment to Christ."[11] For this reason, "Our apologetic to the postmodern world needs to emphasize an inclusive community that welcomes in others so that they can observe the reality of the Christian faith."[12]

Missionaries to Cyberland

If we are to be effective as missionaries on the Internet, we must understand the Internet culture. We must understand that, generally speaking, N-Geners value community more than do their boomer parents, and they are willing to seek and create community in this virtual world. We must understand that Internet evangelism will require a significant investment of our time. Building community is a time-consuming process, but it is worthwhile. "Hit-

and-run" evangelism won't cut it with these kids. They've heard enough sales pitches in their young lives; they don't need another come-on for another product, which, to many N-Geners' way of thinking, is exactly what Christianity is. N-Geners crave something real. In fact, they're more interested in the reality—a gut-level, visceral reality—of the gospel than in propositional truth. The key question for N-Geners is not "Is it true?" but "Is it real?"[13]

If missionaries are to be effective emissaries for Christ, they must learn the culture and customs of the groups to whom they minister. As one experienced missionary explains, "We must love the people to whom we minister so much that we are willing to enter their culture as children, to learn how to speak as they speak, play as they play . . . study what they study, and thus earn their respect and admiration."[14] The same principle should apply for those of us who wish to reach out to the lost on the Net. We must immerse ourselves in cyberculture, understanding its customs, its language, and its worldview, before we attempt to share our own worldview in this strange new cyberworld. For any e-vangelist to venture out into the Internet before gaining a good understanding of the culture and customs of cyberspace would be arrogant—just as it would be arrogant for a missionary to expect to minister amid a culture and people about which he or she knows nothing.

To be salt and light in this new medium, believers should approach Internet evangelism in the same way that a farmer approaches planting: first by *cultivating* relationships with nonbelievers on the Net, then by *sowing* the seed of the gospel in the hearts of these nonbelievers through the communication of revelation, and finally by *reaping* the fruit of the witnessing labors.[15] E-vangelism will not be as easy or as instant as logging on to the Net. It will be a process that requires forethought, planning, much study, and, above all, prayer. As Joe Aldrich explains, "Evangelism is gift-driven. Some are great cultivators. Some are gifted sowers. Others are gifted reapers."[16] All phases of the evangelism process are necessary. On the Net, you might connect with people who have already been "cultivated"—the hard, unfertile soil of their hearts has already been broken up by Christians who touched their lives before you—and you might be the person to sow the Word into their lives. Or you might be the one to "reap" the fruit of another e-vangelist's labors by leading someone in an online prayer for salvation. Or you might be involved in the hard work of cultivating, while others will later sow and reap where you have already made your contribution.

Cultivating, sowing, and reaping are all equally important parts of the evangelism process. Who sows and who reaps is not important. What matters is that a soul is saved, and that the process of evangelism—not an instant, single event, but a process—has borne fruit. Only then can we truly expect to make digital disciples.

*e*Connections: Online Resources for *e*Ministry

Start Spreading the News

One of the most comprehensive guides to Internet evangelism is Tony Whittaker's Web Evangelism Guide (www.web-evangelism .com). Another is David Campbell's search engine/directory, Fishthe.Net (www.fishthe.net). Visit both these resources for helpful e-vangelism tips.

The Lambs That Roared

Plug into the "Roaring Lambs" Web site (www.roaringlambs.net) and listen to the song "Out There," by Steven Curtis Chapman and Michael W. Smith. What does the song have to say about sharing the gospel in cyberspace?

The Harvest Is Great. . . .

Visit Greg Laurie's "Harvest Online" (www.harvest.org) and consider how this site connects the Harvest Crusades with cyberculture. What is it about this Web site that might hold the attention of online seekers?

The Cybersaints "Strike" Back

For insight into chat room evangelism, visit the home base of STRIKE, an Internet chat ministry, at www.strike.someone.net.

E-vangelize Your Church Web Site

The Southern Baptist Convention's North American Mission Board (NAMB) has created a free downloadable gospel presentation to help local churches become more evangelistic online. Download the Internet Evangelism Kit for your church Web site at www.namb.net/evangelismkit/default.htm. (The NAMB is serious about online evangelism; in 2000 the board hired its first full-time "cyber missionary.")

CHAPTER TWELVE

Making Digital Disciples

> *Go therefore and make disciples of all the nations, baptizing them in the name of the Father and of the Son and of the Holy Spirit, teaching them to observe all things that I have commanded you; and lo, I am with you always, even to the end of the age. Amen.*
> *—Matthew 28:19–20 NKJV*

AS THE FIRST WAVES OF THE Net Generation come crashing into the shores of our culture, many people in the church are bewildered about how to minister to these young people. We aren't sure how to "make disciples" among members of this new generation. Throughout the ages, the church has emphasized the Great Commission mandate of Matthew 28:19 as the foundation for discipleship. But to some observers of this postmodern generation, the Great Commission no longer seems to be the right approach. Or at least, to some observers' way of thinking, it shouldn't be the sole approach to making disciples.

Jesus' Great Commission mandate to make disciples "resonated in the enlightenment era," writes *Generating Hope* author Jimmy Long, because it "is centered around truth (teaching) and self (disciples), and it implies a view of human progress."[1] The baby boom generation, as well as the pre-World War II "builder" generations before them, welcomed the idea of progress. They also were comfortable with modern ideas of objective and absolute truth.

N-Geners, however, are a different breed. More pragmatic and less "idea"-listic than previous generations, they're more likely to be interested in a truth that can be experienced rather than one that is abstract. They prefer hands-on experience to something merely talked about or argued over. Moreover, N-Geners live in a time in which the notion of progress is suspect. Industrial "progress" has resulted in deforestation, ozone depletion, and global environment problems; economic "progress" in the industrialized nations has led to economic exploitation of developing nations; and social "progress"— from Franklin Roosevelt's New Deal to Lyndon Johnson's Great Society—has given rise to the welfare state. N-Geners also live in a time in which people no longer discern "truth" as absolute but as negotiable, as preferences. The great ideas of the Great Commission no longer resonate in a world in which truth is negotiable.

In light of our contemporary condition, perhaps the church should seriously consider Long's contention that "a new mandate might be needed for the postmodern era."[2] Long suggests that the church need not dismiss the Great Commission altogether but place a renewed emphasis on another "great" mandate that Jesus left the church, the Great Commandment:

> "Love the Lord your God with all your heart and with all your soul and with all your mind." This is the first and greatest commandment. And the second is like it: "Love your neighbor as yourself." All the Law and the Prophets hang on these two commandments.
> —Matthew 22:37–40 NIV

"The Great Commandment," Long writes, "focuses on relationships (neighbor) and community It implies human frailty or misery, which need a loving environment. It also implies the presence of God in the process. Humankind is not left to its own initiative."[3]

As we have already seen, the Net Generation seeks community.

Many people are logging on to cyberspace in search of relationships that they are not finding in their physical surroundings. Through the Net, the church has an opportunity to provide a loving, nurturing cybercommunity for these young people. Through this context of a loving community, the church can take advantage of the online environment as a means to lead these young people into committed discipleship—digital discipleship.

The Dynamics of Discipleship

What is it, exactly, that the church is seeking to accomplish in this quest to make disciples? It is nothing less than the birthing of Christlikeness in those whom we in the church seek to disciple. Jesus calls us to teach new believers to observe His teachings (Matt. 28:20 NKJV). We are to continue in the footsteps of the apostle Paul, who calls upon us to follow his example, just as he follows the example of Christ (1 Cor. 11:1 NIV). The *Evangelical Dictionary of Biblical Theology,* published by Baker Book House, identifies the following three goals of discipleship:[4]

- *Toward Self: Becoming Like Christ.* "The process of becoming like Jesus brings the disciple into intimate relationship with the Lord Jesus Christ, and, as such, is the goal of individual discipleship." In our discipleship of N-Geners, instructing and leading them in Bible study to help them become more Christlike fulfills the Great Commission mandate to make disciples, or "learner-followers."
- *Toward Others: Servanthood.* "In a classic interaction with two of his disciples who were seeking positions of prominence, Jesus declares that servanthood is to be the goal of disciples in relationship to one another (Mark 10:35–45)." Through this servanthood, the Christian displays the love and desire for true community that is identified in the Great Commandment.
- *Toward the World: The Great Commission.* "Through his Great Commission Jesus focuses his followers on the ongoing importance of discipleship through the ages, and declares the

responsibility of disciples toward the world." To "make disciples," *Evangelical Dictionary of Biblical Theology* notes, is evangelistic in nature. It is "to proclaim the gospel message among those who have not yet received forgiveness of sins." And so by reaching out to the non-Christian, we in the church are fulfilling another aspect of Christ's Great Commission.

True discipleship, then, embodies not only the Great Commission mandates of teaching and ultimate, objective truth but also the Great Commandment mandates of love and community. The Great Commandment directs us to relate to N-Geners in a postmodern context. At the same time, we must never lose sight of the Great Commission mandate to lead this generation beyond human fellowship and community to ultimate fellowship and communion with God. As the apostle John explained, "truly our fellowship is with the Father and with His Son Jesus Christ" (1 John 1:3 NKJV).

Writing about Xers, who share similar traits with their younger brothers and sisters, Tom Beaudoin says that generation's concept of discipleship is more focused on community and experience than on the individuality that boomers often emphasize. By "serving others, displaying a commitment to community, building the scriptural reign of God"—what he calls "the practice of discipleship"—Xers will "encounter a living, undomesticated Jesus,"[5] rather than a watered-down version of Jesus that some churches might preach. These same experiential practices will lead N-Geners to encounter a Christ about whom they might never hear in Sunday school.

The challenge to the church, then, is to lead the Net Generation to this "living, undomesticated Jesus" through a process that involves becoming like Christ in thought and lifestyle, serving others, and being witnesses to the world of God's life-transforming power, all in the context of community (in some cases, virtual community).

In the church, we often are tempted to initiate programs to address each of these concepts separately and distinctly. Instead, we should strive to integrate them into a lifestyle of discipleship that involves "learning-following" the example set by Christ.

Dirk C. van Zuylen, a Dutch missionary for the Navigators, warns us against the temptation to treat these discipleship concepts as separate entities. He suggests that we focus not on discipleship programs but on discipleship "dynamics"—or "principles that bring about progress." In particular, we should strive to emulate the four dynamics that drove Jesus' discipleship: truth, love, relevance, and faith.[6]

- *Truth.* As van Zuylen points out, and as we have seen in previous chapters, Jesus often taught in parables, using the common language of the day, to reveal truth to His disciples. "Jesus' mission to save a lost world depended on teaching a few followers the truth and helping them to understand, believe, and apply what He taught."[7] To apply this dynamic in a context of digital discipleship, we in the church should use the power of story to spread God's truth in cyberspace. Online testimonies, such as those discussed in chapter 10, can greatly enhance our Net ministry efforts. The online testimonies of Web communities like Hopenet, for instance, can communicate great truths to a generation seeking spiritual guidance in front of a computer monitor. Also, communicating the truth of God's Word through online Scripture resources— whether virtual Bibles and Bible studies, video clips, or chat room scripts—is a necessary component of introducing the truth to N-Gen seekers in the online environment.
- *Love.* Jesus demonstrated His love in many ways and to many people. So should we. When we are online, we should always "speak the truth in love" (Eph. 4:15 NKJV) and follow Christ's example of putting others before ourselves. As the apostle Paul explained in his first letter to the Corinthians, even if he worked the greatest of miracles, demonstrated faith enough to move mountains, and gave away everything he owned, it would amount to nothing if it were done without love (13:1–3 NKJV). Similarly, in cyberspace we could design the greatest Web sites, offer persuasive chat room arguments for converting to Christianity, and quote Scripture without the help of a Bible bot—but unless we are motivated by the love of God, then it

is all for naught. To demonstrate the love of God online, let us follow Paul's admonition to the Philippians: "Don't be jealous or proud, but be humble and consider others more important than yourselves. Care about them as much as you care about yourselves and think the same way that Christ Jesus thought" (Phil. 2:3–4 CEV).

- *Relevance.* Christians are famous for their irrelevance. We speak in Christian clichés that have no meaning to non-Christians. When we speak of theological concepts such as *salvation, atonement, justification,* and *sanctification,* more often than not we draw little more than blank stares from our audience. If we're irrelevant online, we're likely to find a seeker suddenly log off from our chat rooms or skip our Web sites in favor of something more engaging. Paul understood the importance of being relevant. That's why he used the imagery of the Isthmian Games to discuss spiritual matters with a Greek culture obsessed with sports entertainment (see 1 Cor. 9:24–27 NKJV). That's why he quoted Greek poets, rather than Old Testament Scriptures, to introduce the concept of God as a father and Christians as His children (Acts 17:28 NKJV). Jesus, of course, was the master at relating spiritual truths in a relevant manner. As we share the gospel with N-Geners, whether online or offline, we must strive to be relevant. Remember, our church Web sites compete with the best that Hollywood and Madison Avenue have to offer. This does not mean that our Web sites need to be as slick as MTV, but we *do* have to know that MTV is the epicenter of youth culture in the United States, and we should know how its programming influences our children. Again, the apostle Paul's philosophy—"I do everything I can to win everyone I possibly can" (1 Cor. 9:22 CEV; see also 1 Cor. 9:19–23)—provides a biblical model for relevance in our cyberministry.
- *Faith.* It is crucial that we understand the importance of relying upon God to accomplish His digital discipleship ministry through us and through this medium. We must not only emphasize the importance of faith and prayer with those we

disciple but also understand the importance of faith and prayer in our own lives. We must realize that apart from Christ, we can do nothing (John 15:5 NKJV). As van Zuylen explains, "Like Jesus, we must pray in faith for those we disciple, and we must depend upon God's Spirit to guide us as we minister."[8] Faith moves mountains. It also breaks down digital walls in cyberspace.

Getting Integrated

These four dynamics of discipleship—*truth, love, relevance,* and *faith*—fuse the Great Commission ideals of truth and teaching with the Great Commandment goals of love and community. Rather than separating these dynamics, however, we should integrate them in our discipleship ministry.

"As I try to disciple through dynamics rather than methods," van Zuylen writes, "I have found a few key questions that help me keep these dynamics in mind. What relevant *truth* do I need to share? How can I express *love* to the person I'm discipling? What are the *circumstances of his life* at the moment? What do I need to pray for him in *faith?*"[9] We would do well to keep these questions in mind as we log on to raise up a generation of digital disciples.

Before we go out into the world of cyberspace to make disciples, we should examine one more aspect about the Net Generation. Today's young people live in a society that is fragmented, disintegrated, and "deintegrated." Into this world, the church—and the Net Generation—has come.

· ·

*e*Connections: Online Resources for *e*Ministry

Online Discipleship

Visit Dan Jenkins' Discipleship.Net Web site (www.discipleship .net) for dozens of articles on discipleship, as well as video and audio clips.

Spiritually Hungry

Listen to the song "We Are Hungry" from the CD "Passion: The Road to One Day." (The song is online at www.worshipmusic.com/spd1740.html.) What does this song say about the spiritual hunger of Jesus' disciples? Do the lyrics reflect your spiritual hunger to follow Christ?

Walking with Jesus

Take a look at "Jesus Walk," an online Bible study developed by Ralph Wilson (www.jesuswalk.com). Peruse some of the writings and consider signing up.

Helping the New Christian

Direct any new Christians you know to New Christian Life Ministries on the Web (www.newchristian.com). The site's "StartUp Studies" section consists of four online Bible studies to help a new convert grow in the faith.

From Deintegration to Reintegration

And they shall build the old wastes, they shall raise up the former desolations, and they shall repair the waste cities, the desolations of many generations.

—Isaiah 61:4 KJV

THE YEAR WAS A.D. 427, and Augustine, the bishop of Hippo, was completing his greatest theological work, *The City of God*. This writing project had consumed fourteen years of his life—fourteen years during which Augustine's homeland, the once-great Roman Empire, fell into ruins. When the city of Rome, the seat of power for the empire, fell to barbarian invaders in A.D. 410, many of the people blamed the Christian faith for the empire's sudden and unprecedented destruction. The gods were angry, Roman pagans claimed, "because they were no longer being worshiped."[1] As their once-stable world disintegrated, many Romans began turning to the old gods—as well as many new ones—for guidance and security in those tumultuous times. As science writer and historian Margaret Wertheim explains, "As secular power dissipated in the ancient empire, more and more people turned to mystical, magical, and religious forms to provide new grounding and guidance in their lives."[2]

Augustine, however, took a different approach; he turned inward. Focusing on his relationship with God, he continued to "contend earnestly for the faith which was once for all delivered to the saints" (Jude 3 NKJV). He continued to work on his masterpiece apologetic for the Christian faith.

The Rome of Augustine's day, an empire in rapid decline, bears striking similarities to the United States of today. Like Augustine's contemporaries, we in the postmodern West "live in a time marked by inequity, corruption, and fragmentation," notes Margaret Wertheim. "Ours too seems to be a society past its peak, one no longer sustained by a firm belief in itself and no longer sure of its purpose. As part of the response to this disintegration, Americans everywhere are looking to religion for new grounding in their lives. . . . Like the late Romans we too are searching for a renewed sense of meaning."[3]

Members of the Net Generation in particular are searching for meaning in cyberspace. Many people fear that as our modern-day empire crumbles into ruins, our children are spending too much time seeking solace on the Net. Some people fear that our children's retreat into this virtual world will further "deintegrate" their lives. By seeking solace in cyberspace, are N-Geners allowing their identities to become as fragmented as the culture and society they inhabit? Will life on the screen become more "real" to the Net Generation than the fragmenting, disintegrating society that surrounds them?

N-Geners are not only faith-surfing on the Internet but also many of them are "identity-surfing," experimenting with different personas or aspects of their selves. They "try on" roles in cyberspace, masquerading in chat rooms and multiuser domains (MUDs). A young man poses as a female in a chat room, experimenting with an unfamiliar gender role. Young women and young men alike transform themselves into fantastic creatures—monsters, elves, ogres, half-human/half-animal creations of their imaginations—in fantasy MUD games. Children pretend to be adolescents, or even adults, when they click on to the Net. Many N-Geners log dozens of hours a week in MUDs, where they escape to fantasy worlds that have moved far beyond the realm of *Dungeons and Dragons,* a popular, precomputer role-playing game of late boomers and Generation X. Some observers of Internet life fear that cybernauts are not only becoming addicted to the medium but also developing "multiple identities" in which their "real lives" are becoming less important, and somehow less *real,* than the virtual identities they create in cyberspace.

While some people feel threatened by this trend, others advocate the development of "multiple" or "parallel" identities. These advocates see cyberspace as a means to liberate us from the tyranny of modernist concepts of identity—the idea that we have singular, integrated identities, rather than the postmodern notion of multiple, disintegrated, negotiable identities.

The multiple-identity concept contradicts the Christian belief that our true identities and life purposes are found through our relationship with Jesus Christ. Christ's identity is unwavering and nonnegotiable. But beyond the concerns raised by the Christian perspective, the notion that we can have many fragmented identities fails to take into consideration other significant offline influences in our lives. Family, environment, and heredity have a lot more to do with shaping our identities than does the computer. As Margaret Wertheim points out, "The notion that we can radically *reinvent* ourselves in cyberspace and create whole 'parallel identities' suggests that the very concept of selfhood is endlessly malleable and under our control."[4] Of course, certain aspects of our identities *are* under our control to an extent, but other aspects aren't. Proponents of multiplicity—and the idea that cyberspace can free us from our earthbound, flesh-and-blood identities—tend to ignore "the enormous amount of psychological shaping and forming" that people undergo through their upbringing, in society, and through genetics.[5]

Role playing in MUDs or chat rooms "is simply not an identity-changing experience."[6] Yet, neither is life in the physical body the totality of real life. We humans are more than the sum of our parts; we are more than flesh and blood. As the Christian faith teaches us, we are also spirit-beings. But each of us, regardless of spiritual beliefs, can—and in fact *do*—extend our lives beyond ourselves. This point is true not only in cyberspace but also in our "real lives."

In cyberspace, we are able to extend ourselves beyond our bodies. In that regard, cyberspace "encourages a more fluid and expansive vision of the one self."[7] In cyberspace, we have the opportunity to extend the "self" to entirely new realms. This kind of extension is nothing new, however. As Margaret Wertheim suggests, "The kinds of self-extensions that occur online also take place in our lives offline."[8] Every letter we write, like every e-mail we send or every chat room conversation we have, carries with it some bit of the self. A little bit of the self "leaks out" in our letters, e-mails, and telephone conversations. "If the self 'continues' into cyberspace, then as I say, it also 'continues' through the post and over the phone."[9]

Reintegrating Our Lives

The challenge to the church in this postmodern cyberworld, as well as to individuals online, is to become "integrated."[10] Or, to put it another way, to become "reintegrated"—moving beyond the "deintegrated" of our fragmented empire to restore wholeness to our lives, our worldviews, and our philosophies.

This is what Augustine did when he wrote *The City of God*. Throughout the history of the Roman Empire, the empire promised its citizens stability and endurance. Yet, in a matter of a few years, the powerful empire, like a house built on shifting sand, fell. All of its seemingly rock-solid stability dissipated. Rome moved from permanence to fragmentation and deintegration.

With *The City of God*, Augustine offered the fragmented empire a new worldview—the first truly Christian view of history, the first major apologetic for the faith, and the foundation for the Western church of the Middle Ages. *The City of God* was born out of late antique Rome's "cauldron of mystico religious fermentation" in which "all manner of sects flourished."[11] Out of the fragmentation of empire was born a theological work that not only addressed the fundamental questions about civil morality and public values but also provided the foundation upon which the Western church would build, for better or worse, its own empire from the ruins of the Roman Empire. It was a reintegration of timeless truths, plucked from the deintegrated debris of the caesars. Today, writes theologian Louis Dupré, "At a time when the unity of our culture has become scattered, we, like Augustine, are forced to rebuild it from within. Augustine's world was more religious than ours. But he shared our predicament of living at a time in which traditional values had collapsed."[12]

For this reason, it is important that our inner lives be fully integrated in sound, solid, Christian faith. During this time of collapsing values, Christians must be firmly "grounded and settled" in the faith, as Paul wrote (Col. 1:23 KJV). For young people especially, the challenge lies in internalizing the truths of the Christian faith as a safeguard against the heresies that flourish in the decaying humus of modernism.

The Internet can help us integrate. It can strengthen our Christian life. But it is not the complete answer. The cyberchurch cannot exist independent of the "real world" church. Neither can the church flourish in this new era without acknowledging the importance and impact of cyberspace on our lives. Internet-based communities *are* as real as our cities, churches, and fraternal lodges. We should not allow cybercommunities to replace the existing Christian communities of the church, but they *can* become extensions of the church into the online world. We should neither reject the virtual world altogether nor strive to escape our physical world by creating some parallel "online" life. Instead, we should strive to integrate the valuable attributes of cyberchurch into our offline lives and our offline faith and values into our online encounters. As writer Donald L. Baker explains, "Cyberspace technologies will not help the millennial generation extract knowledge and wisdom from data if they are not *taught* to recognize that some ideas are more important than others and some are, in fact, true and worth emulating. Internalizing the teachings of the Bible, for example, will be far more useful for life than any number of database 'hits' without context or underlying values."[13]

As a new medium for extending the self, however, the Internet continues a tradition of Christian outreach that has existed since the church's earliest days. The early Christians were known for meeting together daily, both in their homes and in the temple (see Acts 5:42 KJV). Many cyber-Christians also meet daily, logging on from their homes into a new kind of temple. Through the Internet, the church is extending into a new realm, creating new outreaches, new relationships, and new opportunities for discipleship.

Net sociologist/philosopher Sherry Turkle aptly summarized the importance of integrating our online activities with our nonnetworked lives.

> We don't have to reject life on the screen, but we don't have to treat it as an alternative life either. We can use it as a space for growth. Having literally written our online personae into existence, we are in a position to be more aware of what we project into everyday life. Like the anthropologist returning home from a foreign culture, the voyager in virtuality can return to a real world better equipped to understand its artifices.[14]

For Such a Time as This

Augustine sifted through the ruins of the shattered Roman Empire and created a work that has endured throughout the church age. Can N-Geners do the same? Will the Net Generation sift through the rubble of their fragmented lives and culture and create something of lasting and eternal value?

I believe they will. Just as God used Esther, a young lady in a strange land and culture, to save an entire people from extinction, so He can use the Net Generation. N-Geners not only can save the Christian faith from disintegration in the seething cauldron of cults and mysticism but also can transform the faith into something vital and vibrant to both their own generation and future generations. Today's Net Generation can build upon the foundation of Christ to advance the faith into the new millennium. Like

Esther, the Internet generation has come into the kingdom for such a time as this (see Esther 4:14).

Just as Mordecai was at Esther's side to remind her who—and whose—she was, so must the church walk alongside the Net Generation as they enter this strange new digital world, a world more familiar to them than to their elders. Yet, as the elders of N-Gen, we too must not forget that we have come into the kingdom for such a time as this.

Internet Resources for Teens and Families

THE FOLLOWING WORLD WIDE WEB sites are recommended as resources to help N-Geners and their parents develop a biblical approach to life in cyberspace. Although not all of the sites listed are specifically Christian in nature, the author considers all of them to be family friendly. With the help of these sites, families will be better equipped to navigate safely and productively the sometimes confusing world of the Internet.

In this era of constant change, online resources appear, disappear, or reappear with a new Web address almost daily. For those who wish to keep up with the ever-changing Christian community online, the Internet for Christians Newsletter (www.gospelcom .net/ifc/) is a necessity. Every two weeks, this electronic newsletter provides updates on what's new in the Christian cyberscene. You can have this free newsletter delivered by e-mail by signing up at the Web site.

Bible Study Tools

The Net contains a wealth of resources for students of the Word. Determining how to mine the Net for those resources, however, can be a daunting task. Following are some links to get you started.

1. Online Bibles

- The Bible Gateway (bible.gospelcom.net). This site from the Gospel Communications Network (www.gospelcom.net) provides nine translations of the Bible in twelve languages. The site's hypersearch function operates like a cyberconcordance, letting you find Scriptures by using keywords.
- Bible Study Tools (www.biblestudytools.net). This site, part of the GOSHEN (goshen.net) and Crosswalk.com (www.crosswalk.com) family of Web sites, allows keyword and Scripture searches of fourteen translations or a metasearch of all available English translations. This site includes links to commentaries, concordances, dictionaries, sermon illustrations, and other helpful resources.
- The NET Bible (www.bible.org/netbible/index.htm). NET stands for New English Translation. This new translation, designed for the Internet, is a project of the Biblical Studies Foundation (www.bible.org).

2. Other Bible Helps and Resources

- The Biblical Studies Foundation (www.bible.org). This site provides Bible studies, sermon illustrations, essays on theology and church history, links to online Bible translations, and more.
- Fresh Sermon Illustrations (www.wsbaptist.com/fsi/). This site was created by Lavern E. Brown Jr., a pastor in Sedona, Arizona.
- GOSHEN (goshen.net). This site provides direct links to news, study resources, devotionals, Christian software, and a Christian-oriented search and directory service.
- Gospel Communications Network (www.gospelcom.net). This consortium of ministries includes links to devotionals,

resources for pastors and youth ministers, news, online Bibles, and a collection of electronic mailing lists devoted to a broad array of Christian topics.

- Internet Youth Group (www.geocities.com/Heartland/Prairie/5083/). This Web site provides information, Bible studies, devotionals, and discussions for teens.
- Leadership University (www.leaderu.com). This site contains articles on dozens of topics written by leading evangelical scholars and ministers.
- Not Just Bibles: A Guide to Christian Resources on the Internet (iclnet.org/pub/resources/christian-resources.html). This comprehensive guide was developed by the Institute for Christian Leadership (iclnet.org).

Christian Directories and Search Engines

Several search engines and directories consist only of Christian Web sites, making the search for Christian content easier.

1. Directories

- About.com's Christianity site (christianity.about.com). About.com's guides use the human touch, personally reviewing and selecting the site's content and links.
- Best Christian Sites Report (www.geocities.com/~lmrenault). This Web site, the creation of Lance Renault, is an online archive of his electronic newsletter. Viewers can subscribe to the e-newsletter from the Web site.
- Best of the Christian Web (www.botcw.com).

2. Search Engines and Indices

- All in One Christian Index (allinone.crossdaily.com).
- ChristianityToday.com (www.christianitytoday.com). The site for the Christianity Today family of magazines includes a search engine.

- ChristianLife (www.christianlife.com).
- CrossSearch (www.crosssearch.com).
- The Crosswalk.com Omnilist (omnilist.crosswalk.com).
- Fishthe.Net (www.fishthe.net).
- GOSHEN (goshen.net).

Christian Communities, General

1. Christian Communities on Internet Relay Chat (IRC)

- Bornagain.net (www.bornagain.net). This Christian IRC network was developed with the help of N-Gener Brandan Kraft (see chap. 8).
- ChristianChat.com (www.christianchat.com). This site provides Web access to Christian-oriented chat rooms on Internet Relay Chat servers.
- CircaNet (www.circanet.org). This organization, which stands for "Christian Internet Relay Chat Association," provides listings of Christian IRC channels on its Web site (ww.circanet.org/chatlist.htm).

2. Web-Based Christian Communities

- About.com's Christianity site (christianity.about.com). News, events, chat, forums, and more, all maintained under the watchful eye of Charles Henderson, founder of the First Church of Cyberspace (www.godweb.org).
- ChristianityToday.com (www.christianitytoday.com).
- Crosswalk.com (www.crosswalk.com).
- Global Christian Network (www.gcnhome.com).
- iExalt.com (www.iexalt.com).
- Jesus Café Ministries (www.jesuscafe.com).
- WorldVillage (www.worldvillage.com). This family-oriented Web community is not explicitly Christian, but provides a Christian-friendly atmosphere.

Christian Communities for N-Geners

- About.com's Christian Teens site (christianteens.about.com).
- ChristianTeens.Net (www.christianteens.net).
- Hopenet (www.hopenet.net). This site is primarily evangelistic in nature but also provides resources and community for new Christians.
- iamnext.com (www.iamnext.com). This site is both a Webzine and an online community for teens.
- Teen Expresso (www.ratedg.com/channels/teens/index.htm), a portal connecting teens to various Christian resources, chat rooms, music and media channels, and more.
- Teens4Jesus (www.teens4jesus.org).
- Yahoo! clubs for Christian teens (dir.clubs.yahoo.com/ Religion___Beliefs/Christianity/Teenagers/).
- ZJAM Youth Ministries (www.zjam.com).

Family and Parental Resources

- America Links Up (www.netparents.org). This site's "Tools and Tips for Parents" (www.netparents.org/parentstips/ index.shtml) provides helpful hints for safely surfing the Web.
- The Center for On Line Addiction (www.netaddiction.com). This site provides a wealth of information on the subject of Internet addiction. COLA's "Kids and Computers—Addiction and Media Violence" (www.netaddiction.com/parents.htm) includes background on how various media, including the Internet, influence children and contains a link to an online Net addiction test.
- Focus on the Family (www.family.org). Focus's "Positive Use of the Internet" Web page (www.family.org/fmedia/infosheets/ a0001974.html) provides tips on ensuring safe surfing for your kids.
- GetNetWise (www.GetNetWise.org). This organization provides more hints for parents as well as links to wholesome Web sites for children, teens, and families.

Filtering Software and Services

- Crosswalk.com's Internet Safety site (www.crosswalk.com/ info/filtering). This site recommends commercially available web-filtering software.
- Parental Control of the Internet (www.worldvillage.com/wv/ school/html/control.htm). This site lists commercially available blocking software and Net-based advocacy groups for safe Web surfing. The list is provided by WorldVillage (www.worldvillage.com), a family-oriented Web community.
- Rated-G Online (www.rated-g.com). Rated-G is one of several Internet service providers that blocks R-rated and X-rated material.

Safe Sites for N-Geners

- GetNetWise's Web Sites for Kids (www.GetNetWise.com/ kidsites/). This listing of wholesome and educational links is a good launching pad for exploring the Net.
- The Gospel Communications Network's sites for children (www.gospelcom.net/welcome/categories/children.shtml). This site provides links to a variety of Christian Web sites for children.
- Kid City Virtual Village (www.child.net/kidcity.htm). This site provides live chat, discussion forums, and links to everything from Beanie Babies to Bill Nye, the Science Guy.
- Kidsurf Online (www.kidsurf.net). Billed as "a Christian Internet surfboard for kids and teens."
- Kidsurfer (www.kidsurfer.org/mail.htm). This site provides free Web-based e-mail for children ages seven to twelve.
- Rated G Kidz (www.rated-g.com/channels/kidz.htm). This site, from the Internet service provider Rated-G Online, provides links to a variety of safe sites.
- Safe Harbors (www.enough.org/safeharbors.htm). This section of the Enough is Enough Web site (www.enough.org) provides links to Web pages for children and parents.

- The Surf Monkey Kids Channel (www.surfmonkey.com) provides fun links for kids as well as a service for safe surfing, called the Surf Monkey Bar.
- Teen.com (www.teen.com). Teen.com is a great starting point for teens' Net explorations.
- TeenCentral.Net (www.teencentral.net). This site provides teen-to-teen peer counseling on a variety of topics. Developed by experts in teen counseling and psychology, TeenCentral also provides an anonymous community for teens to engage in online chat and discussion.
- Ultimate Veggie (www.ultimateveggie.com). Bob, Larry, and all of the other VeggieTales pals are here.
- WorldVillage (www.worldvillage.com), an online community for all ages.

Notes

Introduction

1. Sherry Turkle, *The Second Self: Computers and the Human Spirit* (London: Granada Publishing, 1985), 325.
2. Heidi Campbell, "Congregation of the Disembodied: A Look at a Religious Community on the Internet" (paper presented to the Sociology of Religion Study Group at the British Sociological Association 1998 Conference, University of Edinburgh, Scotland, 9 April 1998).
3. One such online chat room modeled after a traditional Christian concept is the Undernet IRC room called *#chapel*. See Andrew Careaga, *E-vangelism: Sharing the Gospel in Cyberspace* (Lafayette, La.: Vital Issues Press, 1999), 119–20.
4. Grunwald Associates. "Children, Families and the Internet 2000." News release, 7 June 2000; www.grunwald.com/survey/newsrelease.html; and Rob Bernstein and David Sheff, "How America Uses the Net," *Yahoo! Internet Life,* September 1999, 114.
5. Sherry Turkle, *Life on the Screen: Identity in the Age of the Internet* (New York: Simon & Schuster, 1995).
6. Matt Donnelly, "Reaching a Wired Generation," *Computing Today,* March–April 1999.
7. Terry Mattingly. "Odds & Sods '99: God, Van Halen & Beyond."

On Religion, 14 April 1999; www.gospelcom.net/tmattingly/1999/col/col.04.14.99.html.

8. "Cyberstats," *Christianity Online,* September–October 1999, 16. The article cites a Survey.net study (www.survey.net/svrlg.html) in which 38.4 percent of all Web users identify themselves as Christians.

9. George Barna, *The Second Coming of the Church* (Nashville: Word, 1998), 5.

10. James Emery White, *Rethinking the Church: A Challenge to Creative Redesign in an Age of Transition* (Grand Rapids: Baker, 1997), 18.

11. Tom Sine, *Mustard Seed Versus McWorld* (Grand Rapids: Baker, 1999), 125.

12. Ibid., 30.

Chapter 1: Wake Up! It's Time for Cyberchurch

1. This identity, like many others described in this book, is not the nickname by which the user goes when online.

2. Private e-mail correspondence between LookingGlass and the author.

3. George Barna, *The Second Coming of the Church* (Nashville: Word, 1998), 65.

4. Barna Research Group, "The Cyberchurch Is Coming: National Survey of Teenagers Shows Expectation of Substituting Internet for Corner Church" (Oxnard, Calif.: Barna Research Group, 1998); www.barna.org.

5. Comments are from the author's online discussions with a focus group of seventeen Christian teens that occurred during July, August, and September 1998.

6. Dawson McAllister, *Saving the Millennial Generation* (Nashville: Nelson, 1999), 11.

7. Andrew Careaga, "The Internet's Impact on Kids' Faith," *Group,* September–October 2000, 94.

8. Electronic message posted to "I Told Someone," an electronic forum at Live the Life Online (www.livethelife.org), 4 September 1998.

9. Brad Stone, "The Keyboard Kids," *Newsweek,* 8 June 1998, 72.

10. Matt Richtel, "Billy Graham's Ministry Explores Cyber Evangelism," *The New York Times,* 4 October 1997 (www.nytimes.com).

11. Ibid.

12. "Cyberstats," *Christianity Online,* September–October 1999, 16.

13. Jimmy Long, *Generating Hope: A Strategy for Reaching the Postmodern Generation* (Downers Grove, Ill.: InterVarsity, 1997), 27.

14. Barna Research Group, "The Cyberchurch Is Coming."

15. Ibid.

16. David Fisher, *The 21st Century Pastor* (Grand Rapids: Zondervan, 1996), 53.

17. Long, *Generating Hope,* 75.

18. Robert Wuthnow, "Religion and Television: The Public and the Private," *American Evangelicals and the Mass Media,* ed. Quentin J. Schultze (Grand Rapids: Zondervan, 1990), 205.

19. Jon Katz, *Virtuous Reality: How America Surrendered Discussion of Moral Values to Opportunists, Nitwits and Blockheads like William Bennett* (New York: Random House, 1997), 55–56.

20. Mark Moring and Matt Donnelly, "Christians in Cyberspace," *Christianity Online,* September–October 1999, 14.

21. The story of how the Internet affected the doctrinal stance of the Worldwide Church of God is detailed in Mark Kellner, "Interlude: The Network That Broke a Church," in *God on the Internet* (Foster City, Calif.: IDG Books, 1996), 129–33.

22. Jeff Zaleski, *The Soul of Cyberspace: How Technology Is Changing Our Spiritual Lives* (New York: HarperEdge, 1997), 111–12.

23. "Gospelcom Reaches Record Level in Traffic for February 1999." *Internet for Christians,* no. 78. (1 March 1999); www.gospelcom.net/ifc.

24. Eric Stanford, *Publishing for Postmoderns: An Introduction for Authors, Editors, and Publishers* (Colorado Springs, Colo.: Stanford Creative Services, 1999), 15 (www.stanfordcreative.com).

Chapter 2: Meet the Net Generation

1. U.S. Department of Education, National Center for Education Statistics. *Projection of Education Statistics to 2007;* nces.ed.gov/NCES/pubs/pj/p97f30.html.

2. Some information for this list was derived from "The List," *UCDA Designer,* Summer 1999, 16; and "What You Should Know About This Year's Freshmen," *The Chronicle of Higher Education,* 3 September 1999, A12. (Both articles are reproductions of a list of char-

acteristics of first-year students entering Beloit College in Wisconsin. "The List" exposes the worldview of freshmen from the fall of 1998, and "What You Should Know About This Year's Freshmen" is the 1999 model.) Other information is from Chris Woodyard, "Generation Y: Boomers' Kids a Booming Market," *USA Today,* 6 October 1998, 1A, and from the author.

3. Don Tapscott, *Growing Up Digital: The Rise of the Net Generation* (New York: McGraw-Hill, 1998), 17–18, 22.

4. Ibid., 1–2.

5. Rick and Kathy Hicks, *Boomers, Xers and Other Strangers* (Wheaton, Ill./Colorado Springs, Colo.: Tyndale House/Focus on the Family, 1999), 279.

6. Wendy Murray Zoba, "The Class of '00," *Christianity Today* 41, no. 2 (3 February 1997); www.christianitytoday.com.

7. Tapscott, *Growing Up Digital,* 78.

8. Kelly McCollum, "Bill Gates Looks Ahead to the Era of 'Generation I,'" *The Chronicle of Higher Education,* 29 October 1999 (chronicle.com).

9. Woodyard, "Generation Y: Boomers' Kids a Booming Market," 1A–2A.

10. Janine Lopiano-Misdom and Joanne De Luca, *Street Trends: How Today's Alternative Youth Cultures Are Creating Tomorrow's Mainstream Markets* (New York: HarperBusiness, 1997), xiii.

11. William Strauss and Neil Howe, *Generations: The History of America's Future, 1514–2069* (New York: William Morrow, 1991), 335.

12. Ibid., 337.

13. Janelle Carter, "Report: Kids Face Critical Threats," The Associated Press, 29 November 1999 (wire.ap.org).

14. Patricia Hersch, *A Tribe Apart: A Journey into the Heart of American Adolescence* (New York: FawcettColumbine, 1998), 165.

15. Polly LaBarre. "What's New, What's Hot." *Fast Company,* no. 21, (January, 1999); www.fastcompany.com/online/21/one.html.

16. Tapscott, *Growing Up Digital,* 21.

17. Nathan Cobb. "Generation 2000: Meet Tomorrow's Teens." *The Boston Globe,* 28 April 1998; www.boston.com/globe/living/packages/generation2000main428.htm.

18. Ibid.

19. Ibid.

20. Tom Sine, *Mustard Seed Versus McWorld* (Grand Rapids: Baker, 1999), 96.

21. Cobb, "Generation 2000."

22. Ibid.

23. Tapscott, *Growing Up Digital*, 212.

24. Ibid., 218.

25. Dawson McAllister, *Saving the Millennial Generation* (Nashville: Nelson, 1999), 8.

26. Dennis McCallum, "Common Ground," *Discipleship Journal* 98 (March–April 1997): 56.

27. Tapscott, *Growing Up Digital*, 287.

28. Zoba, "The Class of '00."

29. Os Guinness, *Fit Bodies, Fat Minds: Why Evangelicals Don't Think and What to Do About It* (Grand Rapids: Baker, 1994), 108.

30. Richard Cimino and Don Lattin. "Choosing My Religion." *American Demographics,* April 1999; www.demographics.com/publications/ad/99_ad/9904_ad/ad990402.htm.

31. David Fisher, *The 21st Century Pastor* (Grand Rapids: Zondervan, 1996), 77.

32. David W. Henderson, *Culture Shift: Communicating God's Truth to Our Changing World* (Grand Rapids: Baker, 1998), 48.

33. Woodyard, "Generation Y: Boomers' Kids a Booming Market," 1A.

34. Douglas Rushkoff, *Coercion: Why We Listen to What "They" Say* (New York: Riverhead, 1999), 202–3.

35. Cecile S. Holmes, "Teens Picking Their Own Places of Worship," *Religion News Service,* 22 May 1999 (www.religionnews.com).

36. Harvey Cox, "Jesus and Generation X," in *Jesus at 2000,* ed. Marcus J. Borg (Boulder, Colo.: Westview Press, 1998), 93.

37. Guinness, *Fit Bodies, Fat Minds,* 110.

38. Cobb, "Generation 2000."

39. Bob Woods. "Kids Outpacing Adults in Web Use." *USA Today Tech Report,* 20 July 1999; www.usatoday.com/life/cyber/nb/nb5.htm.

40. Stacy Lawrence, "The Net World in Numbers," *The Industry Standard's Metrics Report,* 8 February 2000 (www.thestandard.com).

41. Cobb, "Generation 2000."
42. McAllister, *Saving the Millennial Generation,* 56.
43. Zoba, "The Class of '00."

Chapter 3: Boomer, Xer, N-Gener

1. Ted Bridis, "The Internet's Fastest-Growing Group: Women over 50," The Associated Press/Nando.Net, 26 August 1998 (www.nando.net).

2. For a more comprehensive look at the differences between these three generations, see Rick and Kathy Hicks, *Boomers, Xers and Other Strangers* (Wheaton, Ill./Colorado Springs, Colo.: Tyndale House/ Focus on the Family, 1999).

3. Jeff Zaleski, *The Soul of Cyberspace: How New Technology Is Changing Our Spiritual Lives* (New York: HarperEdge, 1997), 236.

4. Leonard Sweet, *SoulTsunami: Sink or Swim in New Millennium Culture* (Grand Rapids: Zondervan, 1999), 242.

5. Douglas Rushkoff, *Cyberia: Life in the Trenches of Cyberspace* (New York: HarperCollins, 1994), 26–27.

6. Tal Brooke, ed., "Cyberspace: Storming Digital Heaven," in *Virtual Gods* (Eugene, Ore.: Harvest House, 1997), 34.

7. Sherry Turkle, *Life on the Screen: Identity in the Age of Internet* (New York: Simon and Schuster, 1995), 77.

8. Winkie Pratney, *Fire on the Horizon: The Shape of a Twenty-First Century Youth Awakening* (Ventura, Calif.: Renew, 1999), 76.

9. Tim Celek and Dieter Zander, *Inside the Soul of a New Generation* (Grand Rapids: Zondervan, 1996), 25.

10. Todd Hahn and David Verhaagen, *Reckless Hope: Understanding and Reaching Baby Busters* (Grand Rapids: Baker, 1996), 121.

11. Celek and Zander, *Inside the Soul of a New Generation,* 35.

12. Ibid., 30.

13. Hicks, *Boomers, Xers and Other Strangers,* 257.

14. Celek and Zander, *Inside the Soul of a New Generation,* 25.

15. Tom Beaudoin, *Virtual Faith: The Irreverent Spiritual Quest of Generation X* (San Francisco: Jossey-Bass, 1998), 11.

16. George Barna, *The Second Coming of the Church* (Nashville: Word, 1998), 77.

17. Hahn and Verhaagen, *Reckless Hope,* 46.

18. Beaudoin, *Virtual Faith*, 13.

19. Barna, *The Second Coming of the Church*, 76.

20. Don Tapscott, *Growing Up Digital: The Rise of the Net Generation* (New York: McGraw-Hill, 1998), 1–2.

21. Barna, *The Second Coming of the Church*, 130–31.

22. Ibid., 185.

Chapter 4: Po-Mo Gumbo

1. Fyodor Dostoevsky, *The Brothers Karamozov*, ed. Edmund Fuller (New York: Dell, 1956), 181–201.

2. Marilyn Manson, "The Beautiful People," on *Antichrist Superstar*, Marilyn Manson (Nothing/Interscope, 1996); Friedrich Nietzsche, *The Antichrist*, trans. H. L. Mencken (1895; reprint, n.p., 1920), available online at www.fns.org.uk/ac.htm.

3. David W. Henderson, *Culture Shift: Communicating God's Truth to Our Changing World* (Grand Rapids: Baker, 1998), 189.

4. The author of the online essay about Dostoevsky might not even be a young woman at all. I first discovered the essay on a young woman's Web page where she indicated that she was the original author of the essay. Later, I discovered the identical essay on a young man's Web site. His site's version of the essay included his byline. The ease with which essays, articles, artwork, and ideas can be plagiarized or replicated on the Internet, and the frequency of such duplicitous actions, further points to the disintegration of traditional values and ethics in the postmodern milieu of cyberspace.

5. Jimmy Long, *Generating Hope: A Strategy for Reaching the Postmodern Generation* (Downers Grove, Ill.: InterVarsity, 1997), 160.

6. Os Guinness, *Fit Bodies, Fat Minds: Why Evangelicals Don't Think and What to Do About It* (Grand Rapids: Baker, 1994), 105.

7. Matt Morginsky, "Grounded," on *Chase the Sun*, The Orange County Supertones (BEC Recordings, 1999).

8. Ibid.

9. Leonard Sweet, *SoulTsunami: Sink or Swim in New Millennium Culture* (Grand Rapids: Zondervan, 1999), 50.

10. David Fisher, *The 21st Century Pastor* (Grand Rapids: Zondervan, 1996), 27.

11. Jewel Kilcher, "Who Will Save Your Soul?" on *Pieces of You* (WEA/Atlantic, 1995).

12. Coleman Luck. "Touched by a Fallen Angel." *The Tongue,* 20 March 1999; www.demonhunter.com/columnist/luck/luckb.html.

13. Linda S. Mintle, "Hollywood Spirituality," *Charisma,* March 1999, 100.

14. Richard Cimino and Don Lattin, "Choosing My Religion." *American Demographics,* April 1999; www.demographics.com/publications/ad/99_ad/9904_ad/ad990402.htm.

15. Ibid.

16. Tom Sine, *Mustard Seed Versus McWorld* (Grand Rapids: Baker, 1999), 125.

17. Todd Hahn and David Verhaagen, *Reckless Hope: Understanding and Reaching Baby Busters* (Grand Rapids: Baker, 1996), 55–56.

18. Tom Beaudoin, *Virtual Faith: The Irreverent Spiritual Quest of Generation X* (San Francisco: Jossey-Bass, 1998), 25.

19. David L. Edwards, *Christianity: The First Two Thousand Years* (Maryknoll, N.Y.: Orbis, 1997), 592.

20. Guinness, *Fit Bodies, Fat Minds,* 104.

21. Daniel J. Adams. "Toward a Theological Understanding of Postmodernism." *Crosscurrents* 46, no. 4 (winter 1997); www.crosscurrents.org/adams.htm.

22. Karen Armstrong, *A History of God: The 4,000-Year Quest of Judaism, Christianity and Islam* (New York: Ballantine, 1993), 305, 349.

23. Lou Whitworth. "Living in the New Dark Ages." *Probe Ministries,* 1996; www.probe.org/docs/darkages.html.

24. Louis Dupré. "Spiritual Life and the Survival of Christianity: Reflections at the End of the Millennium." *Crosscurrents* 48, no. 3 (fall 1998); www.crosscurrents.org/dupre.htm.

25. Paul Lakeland. "Does Faith Have a Future?" *Crosscurrents* 49, no. 1 (spring 1999); www.crosscurrents.org/lakeland.htm.

26. Dupré, "Spiritual Life and the Survival of Christianity."

27. Ibid.

28. Tal Brooke, ed., "Cyberspace: Storming Digital Heaven," in *Virtual Gods* (Eugene, Ore.: Harvest House, 1997), 35.

29. Larry Wall, "Perl, the First Postmodern Computer Language" (speech

delivered at the Linux World Conference, San Diego, Calif., 3 March 1999); kiev.wall.org/~larry/pm.html.

30. Sherry Turkle, *Life on the Screen: Identity in the Age of the Internet* (New York: Simon & Schuster, 1995), 18, 43.

31. Eric Stanford, *Publishing for Postmoderns: An Introduction for Authors, Editors, and Publishers* (Colorado Springs, Colo.: Stanford Creative Services, 1999), 4; www.stanfordcreative.com.

32. Jeff Zaleski, *The Soul of Cyberspace: How New Technology Is Changing Our Spiritual Lives* (New York: HarperCollins, 1997), 248.

33. Leslie Miller, "Can the Internet Save Souls?" *USA Today*, 30 September 1997, 14D.

34. Beaudoin, *Virtual Faith*, 57.

35. Andrew Careaga, "Pastors in Cyberspace," *Ministries Today*, January–February 1997, 42.

36. Tim Stafford, "Kevin Vanhoozer: Creating a Theological Symphony," *Christianity Today* 43, no. 2 (9 February 1999): 39.

37. Long, *Generating Hope*, 206–7.

38. Sweet, *SoulTsunami*, 133.

39. Ibid., 49.

Chapter 5: Religion, Politics, and Sausage-Making

1. Michelle V. Rafter, "The E-mail Business Is Booming," Reuters News Service, *St. Louis Post-Dispatch*, 5 February 1997, 8C.

2. Ted Bridis, "The Internet's Fastest-Growing Group: Women over 50," The Associated Press/Nando.Net, 26 August 1998 (www. nando.net).

3. Shelley Morrisette, "The Digital Decade: Where Are Consumers Going?" Forrester Research, Inc., 1999 (www.forrester.com).

4. Bridis, "The Internet's Fastest-Growing Group."

5. Reuters News Service, "Internet Now a Necessity, Says Study," 4 December 1998 (www.news.com).

6. James L. McQuivey, with Michael E. Gazala, Gordon Lanpher, and Tell Metzger, "The Net-Powered Generation," Forrester Research, Inc., August 1999 (www.forrester.com).

7. Ibid.

8. Mark A. Kellner, *God on the Internet* (Foster City, Calif.: IDG Books, 1996), 29.

9. Andrew Careaga, *E-vangelism: Sharing the Gospel in Cyberspace* (Lafayette, La.: Vital Issues Press, 1999), 46–47.

Chapter 6: Cyberspace: Land of Peril, Land of Promise

1. Clay Renick, "Internet Affects Church in Small-Town America," *Baptist Press,* 8 September 1997 (www.baptistpress.org).
2. Rose Pike. "Log On, Tune In, Drop Out: New Survey Shows Some Can't Handle Net." ABCNEWS.com, 23 August 1999; abcnews.go .com/sections/living/DailyNews/netaddiction032699.html.
3. Lauren Gibbons Paul, "Who Are Your Teens Talking To (And Why Should You Care)?" *Family PC,* March 1999 (www.familypc.com).
4. The Associated Press, "Study: Internet 'Addicts' Often Show Other Disorders," 31 May 1998, CNN Interactive (cnn.com).
5. Paul, "Who Are Your Teens Talking To?"
6. Associated Press, "Study: Internet 'Addicts' Often Show Other Disorders."
7. Paul, "Who Are Your Teens Talking To?"
8. Tal Brooke, ed., "Lost in the Garden of Digital Delights," in *Virtual Gods* (Eugene, Ore.: Harvest House, 1997), 172.
9. Ibid., 171.
10. Brooks Alexander, "Virtuality and Theophobia," in *Virtual Gods,* 165.
11. Andrew Careaga, "Get Ready for E-vangelism," *Charisma,* June 1997, 53.
12. Ibid., 55, 87.
13. Douglas Groothuis, *The Soul in Cyberspace* (Grand Rapids: Baker, 1997), 142.
14. Andrew Careaga, *E-vangelism: Sharing the Gospel in Cyberspace* (Lafayette, La.: Vital Issues Press, 1999), 133–34.
15. Ben Greenman, "Liar, Liar," *Yahoo! Internet Life,* March 1999, 89–90.
16. David Streitfeld, "A Web of Workaholic Misfits? Study Finds Heavy Internet Users Are Socially Isolated," *Washington Post,* 16 February 2000 (www.washingtonpost.com).
17. Tal Brooke, ed., "Cyberspace: Storming Digital Heaven," in *Virtual Gods,* 27.
18. John Leland, "The Secret Life of Teens," *Newsweek,* 10 May 1999, 48.

19. David Shenk, *Data Smog: Surviving the Information Glut* (San Francisco: HarperEdge, 1997), 31.

20. eMarketer. "Information Haves and Haves Not." *eStats,* 12 July 1999; www.emarketer.com/estats. The U.S. Department of Commerce's National Telecommunications and Information Administration Report, "Falling Through the Net: Defining the Digital Divide," was released 8 July 1999 and is available online at www.ntia.doc.gov/ntiahome/digitaldivide/.

21. Bill Gates, *The Road Ahead* (New York: Viking, 1995), 134.

22. David Sarnoff, foreword to *Television Broadcasting,* by Lenox R. Lohr (New York: McGraw-Hill, 1940), cited in Shenk, *Data Smog,* 60.

23. Shenk, *Data Smog,* 60.

24. Donna Rice Hughes and Pamela T. Campbell, *Kids Online: Protecting Your Children in Cyberspace* (Grand Rapids: Revell, 1998), 52.

25. Walt Mueller, *Understanding Today's Youth Culture* (Wheaton, Ill.: Tyndale House, 1994, 1999), 175.

26. Jon Katz, *Virtuous Reality: How America Surrendered Discussion of Moral Values to Opportunists, Nitwits and Blockheads Like William Bennett* (New York: Random House, 1997), 182–92.

27. Focus on the Family, "Positive Use of the Internet" (www.family.org/fmedia/infosheets/a0001974.html); America Links Up, "Tools and Tips for Parents" (www.netparents.org/parentstips/index.shtml). See also Mueller, *Understanding Today's Youth Culture,* 202–4.

Chapter 7: Bibles, Bots, and Body Art

1. The reference is to multitattooed Henry Rollins, former lead singer for the punk rock band Black Flag and the Rollins Band.

2. Partial text from a chat in the Internet Relay Chat channel *#Teens4Christ,* 20 October 1998. The original nicknames of the chatters have been changed.

3. Evangelical Press News Service, "Move Over WWJD Bracelets—Christian Tattoos?" *Maranatha Christian Journal,* 25 March 1999 (www.mcjonline.com).

4. Tom Beaudoin, *Virtual Faith: The Irreverent Spiritual Quest of Generation X* (San Francisco: Jossey-Bass, 1998), 78.

5. Evangelical Press News Service, "Move Over WWJD Bracelets—Christian Tattoos?"

6. *WWJD* stands for "What Would Jesus Do?" and grew out of a movement started by a church youth group in Michigan as the members studied Charles Sheldon's book *In His Steps,* published in 1896. The movement spawned a Christian fashion revolution, resulting in all manner of WWJD apparel and accessories, a WWJD album, and even a WWJD board game (Bo Cassell, "What Would Jesus Think of WWJD?" *Group* 25, no. 3 [March–April 1999]: 30–31). *FROG,* which stands for "Fully Rely on God," came about as a reaction to the WWJD phenomenon and quickly became a trend in its own right.

7. On two separate occasions, once in December 1998 and again in April 1999, I submitted a question about body modification to Christian Answers Net. At this writing, nothing on the topic has been posted to the Web site.

8. Jon Katz, review of *The Pearly Gates of Cyberspace,* by Margaret Wertheim, *Slashdot,* 19 April 1999 (slashdot.org/books/99/04/13/195259.shtml). Margaret Wertheim, *The Pearly Gates of Cyberspace: A History of Space from Dante to the Internet* (New York: W. W. Norton & Co., 1999).

9. Rick Bauer, the leader of Freedom House Ministries, quoted in Terry Mattingly, "The Web, the Cults and the Church." *On Religion,* 2 April 1997; www.gospelcom.net/tmattingly.

10. Chris Tauber. "Your Tattoo IQ." react.com, 14–21 November 1999; www.react.com/quiz_central/tattoo/.

11. Paul-Gordon Chandler., "Opening the Book 'Starbucks Style.'" *Light Magazine,* fall 1998; www.gospelcom.net/ibs/light/ed6/.

Chapter 8: The Word on the Web

1. Polly LaBarre. "What's New, What's Hot." *Fast Company,* no. 21 (January 1999); www.fastcompany.com/online/21/one.html.

2. Rodolpho Carrasco, "A Twenty-First-Century Identity Crisis," *Sojourners,* November 1994, 16; cited in Tom Beaudoin, *Virtual Faith: The Irreverent Spiritual Quest of Generation X* (San Francisco: Jossey-Bass, 1998), 93.

3. Paul-Gordon Chandler. "Opening the Book 'Starbucks Style.'" *Light Magazine,* fall 1998; www.gospelcom.net/ibs/light/ed6/.

4. Os Guinness, *Fit Bodies, Fat Minds: Why Evangelicals Don't Think and What to Do About It* (Grand Rapids: Baker, 1994), 95.

5. Leonard Sweet, *SoulTsunami: Sink or Swim in New Millennium Culture* (Grand Rapids: Zondervan, 1999), 200.

6. Beaudoin, *Virtual Faith,* 156.

7. Chandler, "Opening the Book 'Starbucks Style.'"

8. Sweet, *SoulTsunami,* 409.

9. Ibid., 410.

10. Chandler, "Opening the Book 'Starbucks Style.'"

11. Charles Ess. "Prophetic Communities Online? Threat and Promise for the Church in Cyberspace," (www.drury.edu/faculty/ess/church/church.html).

12. Partial text from a chat in the Internet Relay Chat channel *#christianhope,* 8 June 1998. The original nicknames of the chatters have been changed.

13. Ess, "Prophetic Communities Online?"

14. Ibid.

15. Eugene H. Peterson, *The Message: New Testament* (Colorado Springs, Col.: NavPress, 1993, 1994), 6.

16. George Barna, *The Second Coming of the Church* (Nashville: Word, 1998), 186.

17. Sweet, *SoulTsunami,* 207.

18. Douglas Groothuis, *The Soul in Cyberspace* (Grand Rapids: Baker, 1997), 68.

19. Ibid., 69.

20. Charles Henderson, "The Emerging Faith Communities of Cyberspace." *CMC Magazine,* March 1997; www.december.com/cmc/mag/1997/mar/hend.html.

21. Beaudoin, *Virtual Faith,* 125–26.

22. Groothuis, *The Soul in Cyberspace,* 146.

23. Sherry Turkle, *Life on the Screen: Identity in the Age of the Internet* (New York: Simon & Schuster, 1995), 275.

24. Jimmy Long, *Generating Hope: A Strategy for Reaching the Postmodern Generation* (Downers Grove, Ill.: InterVarsity, 1997), 150.

Chapter 9: Virtual Community

1. Andrew Careaga, *E-vangelism: Sharing the Gospel in Cyberspace* (Lafayette, La.: Vital Issues Press, 1999), 128.
2. George Barna, *The Second Coming of the Church* (Nashville: Word, 1998), 19.
3. Richard Cimino and Don Lattin. "Choosing My Religion." *American Demographics,* April 1999; www.demographics.com/publications/ad/99_ad/9904_ad/ad990402.htm.
4. *Center for Parent/Youth Understanding Newsletter,* cited in "Net Heads," *Group,* September–October 1998, 98. The Cheskin Masten imageNet survey of 258 teens found that they spend 1.8 hours a week using the Net for schoolwork and 5.6 hours Web-surfing, 4.9 hours chatting, 3.6 hours on e-mail, 3.1 hours playing games, and 2.2 hours on music-related activities.
5. A survey of Christian teens who use the Internet found that half of them consider their online friendships to be "as real, as close, as important" as non-Internet friendships (Andrew Careaga, "The Internet's Impact on Kids' Faith," *Group,* September–October 2000, 94).
6. Jimmy Long, *Generating Hope: A Strategy for Reaching the Postmodern Generation* (Downers Grove, Ill.: InterVarsity, 1997), 82.
7. Margaret Wertheim, *The Pearly Gates of Cyberspace: A History of Space from Dante to the Internet* (New York: W. W. Norton & Co., 1999), 289–90.
8. Ibid., 290.
9. Howard Rheingold, *The Virtual Community: Homesteading on the Electronic Frontier* (San Francisco: HarperPerennial, 1994), 24; cited in Wertheim, *The Pearly Gates of Cyberspace,* 284.
10. Jon Katz, "Voices from the Hellmouth," *Slashdot,* 26 April 1999 (slashdot.org).
11. Ibid.
12. Douglas Groothuis, *The Soul in Cyberspace* (Grand Rapids: Baker, 1997), 125.
13. Ibid., 143.
14. Brittney G. Chenault. "Developing Personal and Emotional Relationships Via Computer-Mediated Communication." *CMC Magazine,* May 1998; www.december.com/cmc/mag/1998/may/chenault.html.

15. Ibid.
16. Mark Galli, "Foiling Technology," *Computing Today*, May–June 1998, 4.
17. Laura Christianson, "Beyond Internet Babble," *Computing Today*, May–June 1998, 12.
18. Careaga, *E-vangelism*, 154.
19. Tom Beaudoin, *Virtual Faith: The Irreverent Spiritual Quest of Generation X* (San Francisco: Jossey-Bass, 1998), 88.
20. Ibid., 90.
21. Barna Research Group, "The Cyberchurch Is Coming: National Survey of Teenagers Shows Expectation of Substituting Internet for Corner Church" (Oxnard, Calif.: Barna Research Group, 1998); www.barna.org.
22. Heidi Campbell, "Plug In, Log On, & Drop Out? The Impact of the Internet on the Religious Community" (paper presented at the British Association for the Study of Religion, 16 September 1998); www.ed.ac.uk/~ewcv24/BASR.html.
23. Careaga, "The Internet's Impact on Kids' Faith," 94.
24. Augustine, *The City of God, The SAGE Digital Library*, ed. Philip Schaff (Albany, Ore.: SAGE Software, 1996), 43.
25. Beaudoin, *Virtual Faith*, 90.
26. Campbell, "Plug In, Log On, & Drop Out?"
27. Chenault, "Developing Personal and Emotional Relationships Via Computer-Mediated Communication."
28. Galli, "Foiling Technology," 4.
29. Leonard Sweet, *SoulTsunami: Sink or Swim in the New Millennium Culture* (Grand Rapids: Zondervan, 1999), 65.

Chapter 10: Cyber Stories

1. Leonard Sweet, *SoulTsunami: Sink or Swim in New Millennium Culture* (Grand Rapids: Zondervan, 1999), 424.
2. Frederick Buechner, *Telling the Truth: The Gospel as Tragedy, Comedy and Fairy Tale* (San Francisco: Harper & Row, 1977), 23–24.
3. Tom Stebbins, *Friendship Evangelism by the Book* (Camp Hill, Pa.: Christian Publications, 1995), 61.
4. Ibid., 61.

5. Text from "Experiencing the Power to Change," 28 October 1999; www.powertochange.com.
6. David Fisher, *The 21st Century Pastor* (Grand Rapids: Zondervan, 1996), 56–57.
7. Andrew M. Greeley, "A Skeptic Converts to the Web," *Yahoo! Internet Life,* April 1998, 64.
8. Sweet, *SoulTsunami,* 425.
9. Ibid.
10. Todd Hahn and David Verhaagen, *Reckless Hope: Understanding and Reaching Baby Busters* (Grand Rapids: Baker, 1996), 101–9.
11. Ibid., 108.
12. Jimmy Long, *Generating Hope: A Strategy for Reaching the Postmodern Generation* (Downers Grove, Ill.: InterVarsity, 1997), 188.
13. Katie N., "Katie's Testimony: One Hour that Changed My Life," Mililani Baptist Youth Testimonies (www.pixi.com/~mysc/youth-testimony.html).
14. Campus Crusade for Christ International, "5 Clicks to Sharing Your Faith," 1998 (www.worldchangers.net/5clicks).
15. Andrew Careaga, "Taking the Gospel to the Web," *Ministries Today,* September–October 1998, 83. Adapted from tips originally written by Eric Elder, proprietor of the Web site The Ranch (theranch.org).
16. Hahn and Verhaagen, *Reckless Hope,* 108.

Chapter 11: Worldwide Witness

1. "Hot Preaching, Cool Music Lead 12,000 to Christ," *Religion Today,* 4 September 1998 (www.religiontoday.com).
2. "Thousands Accept Christ at Anaheim Greg Laurie Crusade," *Religion Today,* 22 August 1997 (www.religiontoday.com).
3. "Hot Preaching, Cool Music Lead 12,000 to Christ."
4. "Cyber Sermon Suggestions and Virtual Evangelism Tactics," Charisma News Service, 5 July 2000 (www.charismanews.com).
5. I first used the terms *e-vangelism* and *e-vangelist* in "Get Ready for E-vangelism," *Charisma,* June 1997, and later in my book *E-vangelism: Sharing the Gospel in Cyberspace* (Lafayette, La.: Vital Issues Press, 1999).
6. "People groups" is a more accurate rendering of the Greek word

ethne, used in Matthew 28:19 and translated as "nations" in the King James Version of the Bible.

7. Tom Stebbins, *Friendship Evangelism by the Book* (Camp Hill, Pa.: Christian Publications, 1995), 65–66.

8. Ibid., 66.

9. Joe Aldrich, *Lifestyle Evangelism* (Sisters, Ore.: Questar, 1981, 1993), 73.

10. Ibid., 75.

11. Jimmy Long, *Generating Hope: A Strategy for Reaching the Postmodern Generation* (Downers Grove, Ill.: InterVarsity, 1997), 208.

12. Ibid., 196.

13. Ibid., 210.

14. Sherwood G. Lingenfelter and Marvin K. Mayers, *Ministering Cross-Culturally* (Grand Rapids: Baker, 1986), 25.

15. Adapted from Aldrich, *Lifestyle Evangelism,* 77.

16. Aldrich, *Lifestyle Evangelism,* 77.

Chapter 12: Making Digital Disciples

1. Jimmy Long, *Generating Hope: A Strategy for Reaching the Postmodern Generation* (Downers Grove, Ill.: InterVarsity, 1997), 196.

2. Ibid.

3. Ibid., 196–97.

4. Adapted from Walter A. Elwell, ed., "Disciple, Discipleship," in *Evangelical Dictionary of Biblical Theology* (Grand Rapids: Baker, 1996), 177; bible.crosswalk.com/Dictionaries/BakersEvangelicalDictionary.

5. Tom Beaudoin, *Virtual Faith: The Irreverent Spiritual Quest of Generation X* (San Francisco: Jossey-Bass, 1998), 169.

6. Dirk C. van Zuylen, "Discipling Like Jesus," *Discipleship Journal* 19, no. 2, issue 110 (March–April 1999): 76–80.

7. Ibid., 78.

8. Ibid., 79.

9. Ibid., 80.

Conclusion: From Deintegration to Reintegration

1. Tony Lane, *The Lion Book of Christian Thought* (Oxford: Lion Publishing, 1984), 45.

2. Margaret Wertheim, *The Pearly Gates of Cyberspace: A History of Space from Dante to the Internet* (New York: W. W. Norton, 1999), 21.

3. Ibid., 22–23.

4. Ibid., 249.

5. Ibid.

6. Ibid., 250.

7. Ibid., 251.

8. Ibid.

9. Ibid.

10. Sherry Turkle, *Life on the Screen: Identity in the Age of the Internet* (New York: Simon & Schuster, 1995), 258.

11. Wertheim, *The Pearly Gates of Cyberspace*, 22.

12. Louis Dupré. "Spiritual Life and the Survival of Christianity: Reflections at the End of the Millennium." *Crosscurrents* 48, no. 3 (fall 1998); www.aril.org/dupre.htm.

13. Donald L. Baker, "Welcome to the Cyber-Millennium," in *Virtual Gods,* ed. Tal Brooke (Eugene, Ore.: Harvest House, 1997), 50.

14. Turkle, *Life on the Screen,* 263.

Bibliography/Webography

Adams, Daniel J. "Toward a Theological Understanding of Postmodernism." *Crosscurrents* 47, no. 4 (winter 1997). www.crosscurrents.org/adams.htm.

Adler, Jerry. "Online and Bummed Out." *Newsweek,* 14 September 1998, 84.

Aldrich, Joe. *Lifestyle Evangelism.* Sisters, Ore.: Questar, 1981, 1993.

Alexander, Brooks. "Virtuality and Theophobia." In *Virtual Gods.* Ed. Tal Brooke. Eugene, Ore.: Harvest House, 1997.

Armstrong, Karen. *A History of God: The 4,000-Year Quest of Judaism, Christianity and Islam.* New York: Ballantine, 1993.

The Associated Press. "Study: Internet 'Addicts' Often Show Other Disorders." CNN Interactive, 31 May 1998. cnn.com.

Augustine. *The City of God. The SAGE Digital Library.* Ed. Philip Schaff. Albany, Ore.: SAGE Software, 1996.

Baker, Derek A. "Finding God Online." *Yahoo! Internet Life,* April 1998.

Baker, Donald L. "Welcome to the Cyber-Millennium." In *Virtual Gods.* Ed. Tal Brooke. Eugene, Ore.: Harvest House, 1997.

Ballowe, Jeff. "Alone Again, Virtually." *Yahoo! Internet Life,* December 1999.

Barna, George. *The Second Coming of the Church.* Nashville: Word, 1998.

Barna Research Group. "The Cyberchurch Is Coming: National Survey of Teenagers Shows Expectation of Substituting Internet for Corner Church" (www.barna.org). Oxnard, Calif.: Barna Research Group, 1998.

Baudrillard, Jean. *The Transparency of Evil.* Trans. Benedict, J. New York: Verso, 1993.

Beaudoin, Tom. *Virtual Faith: The Irreverent Spiritual Quest of Generation X.* San Francisco: Jossey-Bass, 1998.

Borg, Marcus J., ed. *Jesus at 2000.* Boulder, Colo.: Westview Press, 1998.

Bridis, Ted. "The Internet's Fastest-Growing Group: Women over 50." The Associated Press/Nando.Net, 26, August 1998 (www.nando.net).

Brooke, Tal, ed. "Cyberspace: Storming Digital Heaven." In *Virtual Gods.* Eugene, Ore.: Harvest House, 1997.

———. "Lost in the Garden of Digital Delights." In *Virtual Gods.* Eugene, Ore.: Harvest House, 1997.

Campbell, Heidi. "Congregation of the Disembodied: A Look at a Religious Community on the Internet." Paper presented to the Sociology of Religion Study Group at the British Sociological Association 1998 Conference, University of Edinburgh, Scotland, 9 April 1998.

———. "Plug In, Log On, & Drop Out? The Impact of the Internet on the Religious Community." Paper presented at the British Association for the Study of Religion, 16 September 1998 (www.ed.ac.uk/~ewcv24/BASR.html).

Careaga, Andrew. *E-vangelism: Sharing the Gospel in Cyberspace.* Lafayette, La.: Vital Issues Press, 1999.

———. "Get Ready for E-vangelism." *Charisma,* June 1997.

———. "The Internet's Impact on Kids' Faith." *Group,* September–October 2000.

———. "Pastors in Cyberspace." *Ministries Today,* January–February 1997.

———. "Taking the Gospel to the Web." *Ministries Today,* September–October 1998.

Carter, Janelle. "Report: Kids Face Critical Threats." The Associated Press, 29 November 1999 (wire.ap.org).

Cassell, Bo. "What Would Jesus Think of WWJD?" *Group,* 25, no. 3 (March–April 1999).

Celek, Tim, and Dieter Zander. *Inside the Soul of a New Generation.* Grand Rapids: Zondervan, 1996.

Chandler, Paul-Gordon. "Opening the Book 'Starbucks Style.'" *Light Magazine,* fall 1998. www.gospelcom.net/ibs/light/ed6/.

Chenault, Brittney G. "Developing Personal and Emotional Relationships Via Computer-Mediated Communication." *CMC Magazine,* May 1998. www.december.com/cmc/mag/1998/may/chenault.html.

Christianson, Laura. "Beyond Internet Babble." *Computing Today,* May–June 1998.

Cimino, Richard, and Don Lattin. "Choosing My Religion." *American Demographics,* April 1999. www.demographics.com/publications/ad/99_ad/9904_ad/ad990402.htm.

Cobb, Nathan. "Generation 2000: Meet Tomorrow's Teens." *The Boston Globe,* April 1998. www.boston.com/globe/living/packages/generation2000/main428.htm.

Cox, Harvey. "Jesus and Generation X." In *Jesus at 2000.* Ed. Marcus J. Borg. Boulder, Colo.: Westview Press, 1998.

"Cyber Sermon Suggestions and Virtual Evangelism Tactics." Charisma News Service, 5 July 2000 (www.charismanews.com).

Dostoevsky, Fyodor. *The Brothers Karamozov.* Ed. Edmund Fuller. New York: Dell, 1956.

Dupré, Louis. "Spiritual Life and the Survival of Christianity: Reflections at the End of the Millennium." *Crosscurrents* 48, no. 3 (fall 1998). www.crosscurrents.org/dupre.htm.

eMarketer. "Information Haves and Haves Not." *eStats,* 12 July 1999. www.emarketer.com/estats/.

Ess, Charles. "Prophetic Communities Online? Threat and Promise for the Church in Cyberspace." www.drury.edu/faculty/ess/church/church.html.

Evangelical Press News Service, "Move Over WWJD Bracelets—Christian Tattoos?" *Maranatha Christian Journal,* 25 March 1999 (www.mcjonline.com).

Fisher, David. *The 21st Century Pastor.* Grand Rapids: Zondervan, 1996.

Galli, Mark. "Foiling Technology." *Computing Today,* May–June 1998.

Gates, Bill. *The Road Ahead.* New York: Viking, 1995.

Greeley, Andrew Men. "A Skeptic Converts to the Web." *Yahoo! Internet Life,* April 1998.

Greenman, Ben. "Liar, Liar." *Yahoo! Internet Life,* March 1999.

Groothuis, Douglas. *The Soul in Cyberspace.* Grand Rapids: Baker, 1997.

Grunwald Associates. "Children, Families and the Internet 2000." News release, 7 June 2000. www.grunwald.com/survey/newsrelease.html.

Guinness, Os. *Fit Bodies, Fat Minds: Why Evangelicals Don't Think and What to Do About It.* Grand Rapids: Baker, 1994.

Hahn, Todd, and David Verhaagen. *Reckless Hope: Understanding and Reaching Baby Busters.* Grand Rapids: Baker, 1996.

Henderson, Charles. "The Emerging Faith Communities of Cyberspace." *CMC Magazine,* March 1997. www.december.com/cmc/mag/1997/mar/hend.html.

Henderson, David W. *Culture Shift: Communicating God's Truth to Our Changing World.* Grand Rapids: Baker, 1998.

Hersch, Patricia. *A Tribe Apart: A Journey into the Heart of American Adolescence.* New York: FawcettColumbine, 1998.

Herz, J.C. *Surfing on the Internet: A Nethead's Adventures On-line.* New York: Little, Brown and Co., 1995.

Hicks, Rick and Kathy. *Boomers, Xers and Other Strangers.* Wheaton, Ill./ Colorado Springs, Colo.: Tyndale House/Focus on the Family, 1999.

Holmes, Cecile S. "Teens Picking Their Own Places of Worship." Religion News Service, 22 May 1999. www.religionnews.com.

"Hot Preaching, Cool Music Lead 12,000 to Christ." *Religion Today,* 4 (September 1998). www.religiontoday.com.

Hughes, Donna Rice, and Pamela T. Campbell. *Kids Online: Protecting Your Children in Cyberspace.* Grand Rapids: Revell, 1998.

"Is It Appropriate for Christians to Practise Body Modification?" *Body Modification Ezine,* 12 January 1996. www.BME.FreeQ.com/news/edit003.html.

Johnson, Steven. *Interface Culture: How New Technology Transforms the Way We Create and Communicate.* San Francisco: HarperEdge, 1997.

Katz, Jon. Review of *The Pearly Gates of Cyberspace.* By Maragaret Wertheim. *Slashdot,* 19 April 1999 (slashdot.org/books/99/04/13/195259.shtml).

————. *Virtuous Reality: How America Surrendered Discussion of Moral Values to Opportunists, Nitwits and Blockheads like William Bennett.* New York: Random House, 1997.

————. "Voices from the Hellmouth." *Slashdot,* 26 April 1999 (slashdot.org).

Kellner, Mark. *God on the Internet.* Foster City, Calif.: IDG Books, 1996.

Kiernan, Vincent. "Some Scholars Question Research Methods of Expert on Internet Addiction." *The Chronicle of Higher Education,* 29 May 1998, A25–A27.

LaBarre, Polly. "What's New, What's Hot." *Fast Company,* no. 21 (January 1999). www.fastcompany.com/online/21/one.html.

Lake, David. "Youth: Next on the Net." *The Standard,* 5 June 2000 (www.thestandard.com).

Lakeland, Paul. "Does Faith Have a Future?" *Crosscurrents* 49, no. 1 (spring 1999). www.crosscurrents.org/lakeland.htm.

Lane, Tony. *The Lion Book of Christian Thought.* Oxford: Lion Publishing, 1984.

Lawrence, Stacy. "The Net World in Numbers." *The Industry Standard's Metrics Report,* 8 February 2000 (www.thestandard.com).

Leland, John. "The Secret Life of Teens." *Newsweek,* 10 May 1999.

Lingenfelter, Sherwood G., and Marvin K. Mayers. *Ministering Cross-Culturally.* Grand Rapids: Baker, 1986.

Long, Jimmy. *Generating Hope: A Strategy for Reaching the Postmodern Generation.* Downers Grove, Ill.: InterVarsity, 1997.

Lopiano-Misdom, Janine, and Joanne De Luca. *Street Trends: How Today's Alternative Youth Cultures Are Creating Tomorrow's Mainstream Markets.* New York: HarperBusiness, 1997.

Luck, Coleman. "Touched by a Fallen Angel." *The Tongue,* 20 March 1999. www.demonhunter.com/columnist/luck/luckb.html.

Mattingly, Terry. "Odds & Sods '99: God, Van Halen & Beyond." *On Religion,* 14 April 1999. www.gospelcom.net/tmattingly.

———. "The Web, the Cults and the Church." *On Religion,* 2 April 1997. www.gospelcom.net/tmattingly.

McAllister, Dawson. *Saving the Millennial Generation.* Nashville: Nelson, 1999.

McCallum, Dennis. "Common Ground." *Discipleship Journal* 98 (March–April 1997).

McCollum, Kelly. "Bill Gates Looks Ahead to the Era of 'Generation I.'" *The Chronicle of Higher Education,* 29 October 1999 (chronicle.com).

McQuivey, James L., with Michael E. Gazala, Gordon Lanpher, and Tell Metzger. "The Net-Powered Generation." Forrester Research, Inc., August 1999 (www.forrester.com).

Miller, Leslie. "Can the Internet Save Souls?" *USA Today,* 30 September 1997, 14D.

———. "Saving Souls in Cyberspace." *USA Today,* 18 November 1997, 4D.

Mintle, Linda S. "Hollywood Spirituality." *Charisma,* March 1999, 100.

Mirapaul, Matthew. "Designers and Developers Recruit for an Online Creative Community." *The New York Times Cybertimes,* 4 June 1998 (www.nytimes.com).

Moring, Mark, and Matt Donnelly. "Christians in Cyberspace." *Christianity Online,* September–October 1999.

Morrisette, Shelley. "The Digital Decade: Where Are Consumers Going?" Forrester Research, Inc., 1999 (www.forrester.com).

Mueller, Walt. *Understanding Today's Youth Culture.* Wheaton, Ill.: Tyndale House, 1994, 1999.

National Telecommunications and Information Administration, U.S. Department of Commerce. "Falling Through the Net: Defining the Digital Divide," 8 July 1999 (www.ntia.doc.gov/ntiahome/digitaldivide).

Nietzsche, Friedrich. *The Antichrist.* Trans. H. L. Mencken. 1895; reprint, n.p., 1920 (www.fns.org.uk/ac.htm).

Paul, Lauren Gibbons. "Who Are Your Teens Talking To (And Why Should You Care?)" *Family PC,* March 1999 (www.familypc.com).

Pike, Rose. "Log On, Tune In, Drop Out: New Survey Shows Some Can't Handle Net." ABCNEWS.com, 23 August 1999. abcnews.go.com/sections/living/DailyNews/netaddiction032699.html.

Pratney, Winkie. *Fire on the Horizon: The Shape of a Twenty-First Century Youth Awakening.* Ventura, Calif.: Renew, 1999.

Rafter, Michelle V. "The E-mail Business Is Booming." Reuters News Service, *St. Louis Post-Dispatch,* 5 February 1997, 8C.

Renick, Clay. "Internet Affects Church in Small-Town America." *Baptist Press,* 8 September 1997 (www.baptistpress.org).

Reuters News Service. "Internet Now a Necessity, Says Study." News.com, 4 December 1998 (www.news.com).

Rheingold, Howard. *The Virtual Community: Homesteading on the Electronic Frontier.* San Francisco: HarperPerennial, 1994.

Richtel, Matt. "Billy Graham's Ministry Explores Cyber Evangelism." *The New York Times,* 4 October 1997 (www.nytimes.com).

Rushkoff, Douglas. *Coercion: Why We Listen to What "They" Say.* New York: Riverhead, 1999.

———. *Cyberia: Life in the Trenches of Cyberspace.* New York: HarperCollins, 1994.

———. *Playing the Future: How Kids' Culture Can Teach us to Thrive in an Age of Chaos.* New York: HarperCollins, 1996.

Schroeder, Ralph, Noel Heather, and Raymond M. Lee. "The Sacred and the Virtual: Religion in Multi-User Virtual Reality." *Journal of Computer-Mediated Communications* 4, no. 2 (December 1998). www.ascusc.org/jcmc/vol4/issue2/schroeder.html.

Schultze, Quentin J., ed. *American Evangelicals and the Mass Media.* Grand Rapids: Zondervan, 1990.

———. *Internet for Christians.* Muskegon, Mich.: Gospel Films Publications, 1996.

Shenk, David. *Data Smog: Surviving the Information Glut.* San Francisco: HarperEdge, 1997.

Sine, Tom. *Mustard Seed Versus McWorld.* Grand Rapids: Baker, 1999.

Stafford, Tim. "Kevin Vanhoozer: Creating a Theological Symphony." *Christianity Today* 43, no. 2 (9 February 1999).

Stanford, Eric. *Publishing for Postmoderns: An Introduction for Authors, Editors, and Publishers.* Colorado Springs, Colo.: Stanford Creative Services, 1999.

Stebbins, Tom. *Friendship Evangelism by the Book.* Camp Hill, Pa.: Christian Publications, 1995.

Stone, Brad. "The Keyboard Kids." *Newsweek,* 8 June 1998, 72–73.

Strauss, William, and Neil Howe. *Generations: The History of America's Future, 1584–2069.* New York: William Morrow and Company, 1991.

Streitfeld, David. "A Web of Workaholic Misfits? Study Finds Heavy Internet Users Are Socially Isolated." *Washington Post,* 16 February 2000 (www.washingtonpost.com).

Sweet, Leonard. *SoulTsunami: Sink or Swim in New Millennium Culture.* Grand Rapids: Zondervan, 1999.

Tapscott, Don. *Growing Up Digital: The Rise of the Net Generation.* New York: McGraw-Hill, 1998.

Terrien, Cordell. "Body Adornment." *Body Modification Ezine,* 26 November 1997. www.BME.FreeQ.com/culture/971207/terrien.html.

"Thousands Accept Christ at Anaheim Greg Laurie Crusade." *Religion Today,* 22 August 1997 (www.religiontoday.com).

Turkle, Sherry. *Life on the Screen: Identity in the Age of the Internet.* New York: Simon & Schuster, 1995.

————. *The Second Self: Computers and the Human Spirit.* London: Granada Publishing Limited, 1985.

Van Zuylen, Dirk C. "Discipling Like Jesus." *Discipleship Journal,* 19, no. 2, issue 110 (March–April 1999).

Wall, Larry. "Perl, the First Postmodern Computer Language." Speech delivered at the LinuxWorld Conference, San Diego, Calif., 3 March 1999 (kiev.wall.org/~larry/pm.html).

Wertheim, Margaret. *The Pearly Gates of Cyberspace: A History of Space from Dante to the Internet.* New York: W. W. Norton & Co., 1999.

Whitworth, Lou. "Living in the New Dark Ages." *Probe Ministries,* 1996. www.probe.org/docs/darkages.html.

Woodyard, Chris. "Generation Y: Boomers' Kids a Booming Market." *USA Today,* 6 October 1998, 1A–2A.

Wuthnow, Robert. "Religion and Television: The Public and the Private." *American Evangelicals and the Mass Media.* Ed. Quentin J. Schultze. Grand Rapids: Zondervan, 1990.

Young, Kimberly. *Caught in the Net: How to Recognize the Signs of Internet Addiction—and a Winning Strategy for Recovery.* New York: John Wiley & Sons, 1998.

————. "Internet Addiction: The Emergence of a New Clinical Disorder." Paper presented to the American Psychological Association, Toronto, Canada, 15 August 1996 (www.netaddiction.com/articles/newdisorder.htm).

Zaleski, Jeff. *The Soul of Cyberspace: How Technology Is Changing Our Spiritual Lives.* New York: HarperEdge, 1997.

Zoba, Wendy Murray. "The Class of '00." *Christianity Today* 41, no. 2 (3 February 1997). www.christianityonline.com.

————. *Generation 2K: What Parents and Others Need to Know About the Millennials.* Downers Grove, Ill.: InterVarsity, 1999.

Subject Index

Scripture Index